ROOM
for
GRACE

Maureen Kenner and Daniel Kenner

SILVER BOOT IMPRINTS

Library of Congress Control Number: 2018904575

ISBN 978-1-7320872-0-0 (pbk)

ISBN 978-1-7320872-1-7 (ebook)

For the angels we all know.

ALLOW

There is no controlling life.
Try corralling a lightning bolt,
containing a tornado. Dam a
stream, and it will create a new
channel. Resist, and the tide
will sweep you off your feet.
Allow, and grace will carry
you to higher ground. The only
safety lies in letting it all in –
the wild with the weak; fear,
fantasies, failures and success.
When loss rips off the doors of
the heart, or sadness veils your
vision with despair, practice
becomes simply bearing the truth.
In the choice to let go of your
known way of being, the whole
world is revealed to your new eyes.

DANNA FAULDS
FROM HER BOOK, *GO IN AND IN*

Maureen Kenner and Room 4 students

"You Held My Hand And Walked Me Out Of The Water"

A Preface from Daniel Kenner

Sometimes I look at the photos of my parents before they were sick to try and find clues of the diseases to come. There's one of them courtside at a Providence Friars basketball game, three days after Valentine's Day. It's a Thursday, a school night, timestamped 9:25 p.m. Mom must have skipped *Survivor*. It's almost a year to the day before Dad's official diagnosis. They look bold and bright. They belong together, they're soulmates. And I cry.

Mom chose "Grace" as her confirmation name and lived by that code. She spent her lifetime as a teacher working with the handicapped, elderly, and disenfranchised. She found her joy and happiness in the joy and happiness of others. "When you put others' needs before your own, it is truly in giving that we receive." She lived like the inspirational banners that adorned the bright walls of her Room 4 classroom and saw possibilities in every field trip, every circle in the sand, every Scattergories game, holiday song, night out for pizza and ice cream sundaes, every grandchild, niece, nephew, student, and family member.

Recently, I was asked a question by the parents of a former student at Mom's school. "Just what was it like growing up as Mrs. Kenner's son?" She worked hard at being my mother.

She recognized the way I gravitated toward the world. Sometimes it meant steering. Sometimes it meant letting go. Most of the time it meant letting Dad and me figure it out together while she remained the support. She never asked to be center stage. She was the bad cop and took one for the team many, many times.

"My dad," I answered, "was my favorite parent."

Dad was a natural storyteller and through that, he became my favorite story to tell. He was my hero. The highest compliment I can give of my dad was he had a son that idolized him. Everything my dad loved, I was determined to love just as much or more.

Mom was my best friend's best friend. It took Dad's early-onset diagnosis to realize just how much she was his advocate, always bringing out the best in him. Their love was a powerful lesson. And then, just four months after Dad's diagnosis, Mom learned she had cancer. Caring for a husband with dementia while undergoing chemotherapy revealed strength like I had never seen. She pushed herself seven more minutes, seven more weeks, seven more months, making opportunities to find heart-shaped rocks in the sand and the littlest of tulips pushing out to the sun. Her spirit shined, empathetic and tough. My parents were at their strongest when faced with conflicts, detours, and personal and professional crossroads. I can remember that strength now very clearly and miss that part of them.

In 2015, the three of us traveled for a week to Bar Harbor, Maine for Thurston's lobster, Westside Café's blueberry pie and to celebrate Mom and Dad's thirtieth wedding anniversary. I feared the inevitable. Wanting to convey my love with a symbolic gesture, I planned and organized an oral history project. I recorded thirty hours of interviews and conversations with my mom from our terrace overlooking Frenchman's Bay.

DANIEL: This is an opportunity to share the lessons of your life, to celebrate, to be present. I want to hear the stories. Here's my first question: what is your motivation to live?

MAUREEN: I love my life. I love that I get to do this with you, that I get to spend time with the people I love. But there's a cog in our wheel that's not functioning and everyone's working twice as hard to pick up the slack. It breaks my heart. I feel guilty that this is the story of your two parents. But I gave you a family grounded in love and laughter and generosity and crazy, loopy, kookiness. We are definitely a very strong family. This is the worst time in my life, but I am still responsible for being, and thinking of myself, in a bigger picture. That was a big part of my parenting. Paul Newman called it "luck." Think of all the bright, beautiful examples at The Hole in the Wall Gang Camp. Some of those kids had rotten luck and he felt compelled to help fix that just a little bit.

I turned her oral history into this book because I wanted to capture her stories that were full of reflection and hope. The book became a commitment I made to my parents, my family, and our legacy. During the first year, I worked from our recordings: transcribing and editing, rewriting and stylizing, weaving and structuring Mom's first person narrative into scenes.

Two weeks before Dad told me he was going to die, four weeks before he actually did, and eight weeks before Mom passed, she and I locked ourselves away in a hotel in Newport, Rhode Island so she could read and collaborate on my first draft, my last Christmas gift to her. "What an overwhelming task," she said on the fourth, and final, morning of the trip. "It's possibly the nicest thing anyone has ever given me. I hope the remainder of the process provides you with a sense of comfort knowing you're creating something that will last after we're gone. I expect you to represent Dad and me with your head held high. Be proud of who you are and where you come from." Her eyes followed the waiter as he came to our table with French toast. "You know, I think that's my student Timothy from the same class as Preston in the early nineties."

"Can't be, Mom. Your mind is just playing tricks on you because we just spent days going through years and years of memories. It's not."

"No, no. That broad square grin. That's him."

He put our plates down in front of us and moved back slowly, eyes wide. "I'm sorry to bother you, but are you Mrs. Kenner?"

"Timothy!"

"I knew it!" he called out. It had been twenty-six years. He couldn't stop smiling. "Wait till I tell the guys! We were just talking about you the other day! When I ride the bus home past our school, I think of those days. Nobody ever forgets Mrs. Kenner!"

As we packed upstairs, Mom said, "A teacher never knows how far her influence goes." She never stopped; she lived until she didn't.

"If Dad died today," I told her two weeks after we returned, "he'd be napping with the sun on his face, Bob Dylan playing in the background, with his wife by his side, whose face he'd recognize anywhere. Dad gave me the power of a good story. His whole life he collected heroes. How lucky am I to have been one of them? And if you died today, you'd be content, feet up, having shared your story and lived your dream."

I needed a cathartic project to keep me close to my parents, to hear their voices, to feel protected. The truth is now almost three years after we started the oral history, I'm afraid to be done. This book has been my armor. And my defeat. Watching my father's mind degenerate while my mother's body did the same was gut-wrenching. But our family also made many happy memories during the dark days. As Mom stood at the end of her career, and ultimately, at the end of her life, it was the lessons she learned from her students over her thirty-five-year career that gave her the strength to live another day. Living optimistically, as a patient and as a caregiver, was a beautiful, imperfect struggle. But for four years, the community rallied behind us, nourishing us with daily visits, leis of orchids, origami cranes, handmade cards, gift boxes, songs, and signs on our lawn. As the seasons change, may you continue to be inspired to do something for someone else. Let that spirit grow. Let it make a difference. You are capable. You are already a success story. Hard work really does pay off. There is room for grace.

Daniel Kenner
New York City
May 2018

FALL

Stage 4

Mary Poppins was my nurse on Day 6. "Pretend you're at summer camp," she joked, encouraging every step I made toward healing and recovery. "We've got a whole bunch of activities for you to choose from."

"But instead of Newcomb and color wars and collecting orange salamanders or dancing to Tommy James and the Shondells," I said, "today's activities at the hospital include pain med management, ice chip crunching, and Dammit! Doll whacking..."

"Don't forget IV pole walking," she teased. "I always know when you're coming because your IV pole is the squeakiest." She tenderly guided me back into bed.

"But instead of early morning skinny dipping," I said, "someone signed me up for the johnny gown flash mob."

That really made her laugh. "I wish all my patients worked like you."

"Well, you help make it easy," I admitted. "I loved sleepaway camp. I'd pack my trunk with stamped stationary and Razzles, pick-up sticks and jacks. And my Magic 8-Ball. My bunkmates and I thought we could predict the future. Go figure. I could never have predicted this." She wrapped a warm blanket around my feet. "One year," I continued, "I was the last camper to be picked up and, on the way home, my sisters teased me that my parents wanted to leave me there."

"That's one of the reasons I love my job here," she smiled. "The staff is a family. We're planning a barbecue together this weekend."

It was August 2013.

Dr. David Sanfred, our family practitioner, walked into my room at 6:45 a.m. and stood at the end of my hospital bed. "Maureen, we're getting ready to send you home soon," he said. And then, "It's time to talk."

It was time to face what I'd avoided all week.

"I'm sorry to tell you, but it's very serious." Though by our family's side for many difficult situations, I'd never heard Dr. Sanfred's tone so methodical. "We thought it was Stage 1 but the cancer metastasized from the colon to your umbilicus and has advanced to Stage 4."

The hospital symphony went silent. I turned my head and watched the early morning sunlight peek through the window. "Is it curable?"

He gave my hand a soft pat. "No, it is not curable."

I heard myself gasp.

I was in a panorama shot. I saw Mary Poppins outside the thin curtain share morning notes with the nurse coming on. They whispered, glanced sympathetically in my direction. I struggled for breath and gripped the Dammit! Doll.

"Will I be able to go back to my classroom?"

"No," he cautioned, "you will not be able to teach right now. But soon. We hope."

The tears kept coming. Mary Poppins came back into the room. She reached out and hugged me gently, with so much affection I could feel her heart break.

Count On Me

I was one of the lucky ones. From a very young age, I felt right at home in a classroom. I was excited about going to school. I relished the rituals and routines, the variety of subjects. I loved raising my hand. I developed much of my confidence and curiosity early on in class. Teaching was a revered profession when I was a child, and my teachers were my childhood heroes. I trusted them and they taught me that if I applied myself, I would develop the tools to succeed, that I had the power to positively affect another life.

At age thirteen, I started to volunteer with children who had learning disabilities. I tagged along with my mom on Sunday afternoons to Children's Village, a home for emotionally disturbed children in Dobbs Ferry, New York. I saw major hardships but enjoyed being with other children and was fascinated by their individual stories. I learned how difficult it was for them not to live with their parents, brothers, and sisters. They lived differently than me, but I felt like I belonged there. I had a sense of purpose.

I graduated from Rhode Island College with a degree in Elementary and Special Education on a Saturday in May, 1979. College was about falling in love a few times, music, friends, and building independence, but mainly I focused on my training at the laboratory elementary school on campus. The more classes I took, and the more students I engaged with, the more I realized my heart was in the classroom. The Monday after graduation, the

Providence School Department called. I never forgot what they asked me: "Can we count on you for the fall?"

"Yes," I said. "You can absolutely count on me for the fall."

~

I became a better teacher when I became Daniel's mother. In 1988, after my two-year maternity leave from the Providence Public School Department, I dropped Daniel at home day care for the first time and felt an enormous sadness that I needed to share the responsibilities of caring for him with another. I entered the classroom again, my first year in Room 4 at Vartan Gregorian Elementary School at Fox Point, carrying a photograph of Daniel for my desk.

Fox Point, tucked in near the end of the East Side overlooking the mouth of the Seekonk River, was one of the oldest neighborhoods settled in Rhode Island, established by Native American families along with Portuguese, Italian, and Irish immigrants. The early neighbors were approached about putting an elementary school by George M. Cohan Boulevard, and the forward thinkers built a one-story, barrier-free, rectangular school building with large windows overlooking the preserved Tockwotton Green Space.

Generations of families attended Fox Point and we remembered and honored the legacy of those who came before us. I was one of the youngest teachers on staff. My colleague in Room 6, who had been a student in the school's very first kindergarten class, called me "Mrs. Rogers" because of my sunny disposition. I was strong-willed but it was always my goal to put on a bright color and a beautiful piece of jewelry, look people in the eye, smile, use good manners, and make it a great day. That first day at Fox Point, with amazing clarity, I realized I had been called to care for each child who was another person's somebody special. I dedicated myself to become the kind of teacher from whom I wanted Daniel to learn. My philosophy was to care for, advocate, promote, and educate all children with a moral compass and strong heart. Unafraid to become involved, to speak up and speak out, I strived to maximize my students' learning potential and to provide their families with the support they needed to lead productive, meaningful lives. I set up Room 4 as an environment where, together, we could thrive and feel confident in our ability to take risks.

DIEGO lived in a shelter for homeless women and their children. "I have been put into the lives of my students for a special reason," I reminded myself. "It is my job to create a home in the classroom, to generate joy, to give love, and to work hard."

The students, giddy with excitement, threw a birthday party for Diego. We spent two days with mini-lessons in Writer's Workshop, creating detailed and delightful cards. As each child read their personal message to Diego, I saw the Principles of Learning, heard the elements of Balanced Literacy, and felt the essentials of character development practiced and internalized. I watched twelve children with varying degrees of social, emotional, academic, and physical handicaps celebrate each other. After reading his card, one of my students, Gabriel, asked, "Can I speak from my head and my heart now, Mrs. Kenner?"

"Absolutely, Gabriel! Go for it!"

Gabriel was a magnificent boy, as close to an angel as I had. He had a rare blood disorder and needed to be absent several days a month to have whole body transfusions. He never complained. He was gentle and an enthusiastic participant. Gabriel and Diego formed an immediate bond. "Well, Diego," Gabriel said with conviction, "I want you to know if you ever need anything, anything at all, you can always count on me."

I learned as much from my students as they learned from me. They reinforced my desire to push for understanding and held the most important roles in strengthening my skills as a lifelong learner. For the next twenty-seven years, the rewards I found in teaching Special Ed — small moments loaded with power and inspiration — prepared me for the life I lived, as resilience, tolerance, empathy, faith in the unknown, maintaining a sense of humor (for sure) and a sense of community all paved a clear path that merged my life inside the classroom with my life outside it. I was on a perpetual search for hope, for optimism, for assurance in a world often filled with fear and uncertainty. By witnessing how the students and their families made difficult decisions through hardships and limitations, challenges and setbacks, grace was revealed.

Noticeably Changing

I came home from school on a September afternoon in 2010 and complained to my husband, Buddy, that the faculty refrigerator was broken. The next day, hustling out of school to escape the heat, my teaching assistant told me, "There is a handsome man waiting by the classroom door." Hot and sweaty, but never wanting to miss an opportunity with a handsome man, I dragged myself down the hall. Buddy was grinning outside of Room 4.

"I got you an early anniversary present! Come look!"

There, in the front of the classroom, was a shiny white mini-fridge. On it was a magnet that read, "*May you always have an angel to watch over you.*"

"I went everywhere," he said. "Target, Walmart, Bed, Bath & Beyond. The college kids cleaned off the shelves. But I went to Benny's and finally found the very last one in the city! I already filled the trays for your ice water. Happy Anniversary, Ro!"

Hoping for a romantic beach getaway or jewelry from Green River Silver Company, I thought, "You got me a refrigerator for our twenty-fifth anniversary?" But then Mrs. Martin, my colleague from Room 7, stopped in to say goodbye and, knowing how I love, *love* my ice water and fresh fruit, sighed, smiled, and said, "That's one of the most romantic things I've ever seen."

She was right.

~

For fourteen successful years, Buddy was the head of the highly-respected Performing Arts program at Nathanael Greene Middle School. "We don't do middle school theater, we do theater," he often exclaimed. At a critical time when funds for the arts were being cut, teaching at Nathanael Greene was a showcase of his strengths: Buddy handled every aspect of budgeting, fundraising, and running and maintaining the auditorium and equipment. Highly motivated, driven by his principles and passion for creative expression, he set the bar really high. His expectations fueled the students and he was constantly enthused by their abilities. Fellow teachers always told me they could spot a child who was in Buddy's class because they were typically confident enough to speak in front of a group and participate in class. Around the neighborhood, kids would shout, "Mr. Kenner! Mr. Kenner! See you tomorrow!"

In 2011, when the Providence School Department began closing art, library, and computer technology programs and laying off much-needed student support staff, teachers and families began the "Save Our Schools" campaign. Nathan Bishop, on the East Side, was reopening as a model green middle school, with a state-of-the-art auditorium. With community support from Providence After School Alliance, Trinity Repertory Company, RISD, and Brown University, it was a theater teacher's dream come true. Throughout the summer, Buddy went through the rigorous application and interview process and talked often about how proud he would be to come full circle—to retire from Nathan Bishop, where he'd taught in the seventies. With years of commendations and exemplary evaluations, Buddy proved to be the best candidate and was hired as the new Performing Arts teacher.

That same year, however, Buddy started noticeably changing. He became angry and irritated. The basic manners and courtesy he'd shown our whole married life disappeared. We had fights like we never had before; there was screaming and slamming doors. Matters were uneasy, unsettled. His nightly glass of Shiraz became two, then three, and sometimes four. He wasn't sharing his feelings and, when he did, they were hostile or convoluted.

Other issues developed that were equally, if not more, distressing. One day, my brother John proudly informed us that his son and daughter-in-law were getting ready to buy a house.

"Who is?" Buddy asked.

"Matt. He's getting ready to buy a house."

"Who is that?" Buddy did not know whom we were talking about. We had just gotten back from Matt's wedding.

Soon after, we went to the beach with Daniel and his lifelong friend, Ollie. Buddy and Ollie went way back. They knew each other from the swim club and Little League; in eighth grade, Ollie was cast as the title role in Buddy's *Dracula* production. Then, Ollie had been one of Daniel's George Washington University freshman year roommates. At the Matunuck Oyster Bar that day, Buddy asked him, "What do they call you?"

Ollie, knowing full well of Buddy's reputation as a trickster, said, "Come on, you know me, Buddy."

"No, I just…what do they call you?" Buddy's eyes were foggy. I knew then that he was genuinely confused.

"They call me Ollie."

"Oh, okay. They call you Ollie."

Ollie leaned toward me. "Am I missing something?"

I didn't know how to respond.

The Rocky Move

Charlotte had cut the Kenner family's hair for almost thirty years. On our nephew David's seventeenth birthday, November 16, 2011, Charlotte was giving Buddy and me a haircut. Buddy, always attentive with thoughtful gestures, would set up his grandmother's cherry wooden chair in the kitchen and get the dingy green beach towel from the cupboard upstairs. Charlotte thoroughly painted my hair blonde to cover the gray that had announced itself when I turned thirty. As we chatted about our students, draped in Charlotte's cape, I felt like a superhero. As if on cue, the phone rang. I picked up the cordless receiver.

"Good evening. This is the Providence School Department. May I please speak with Mr. Jacob Kenner?" Surprised that my husband's former principal, and interim Director of Human Resources, was calling at home, I eagerly handed Buddy the phone. A blob of blonde splotched the white receiver. "How wonderful," I thought, "I bet he's calling to announce an award!"

"Hello, this is Jacob Kenner." A puzzled, then downright disturbed look spread across his face. Suddenly, my cape was hot and strangling. "What are you saying...What do you mean...That's impossible...Please, I need more information...Okay...Okay...I'll call the union tomorrow. Goodbye."

The phone slipped out of his hand. A complaint had been lodged and Buddy was on administrative leave, effective immediately. He was ordered not to show up at Nathan Bishop or to speak about this conversation to anyone. It landed like a punch to the back of the head. We were mortified at how the school department handled themselves: we did not learn the allegation for four months, and the administration at Nathan Bishop never provided any compassion or accountability.

The Teacher's Union, with full support from the state, had established a new, exhaustive evaluation process. In the one quarterly observation Buddy did have at Nathan Bishop, he earned a commendable review. The dysfunction of the school system reared its ugly head. We were caught in the crossfire of an explosive situation that didn't have to happen: a brand-new school with a handpicked staff, a rigorous teacher evaluation process, and an active union that could have offered support, but instead we were told to be quiet. The secrecy was ruining the Kenner reputation and causing damage to our family. I cried every day. I wanted Buddy to fight but he was full of doubt. In this dark and dreadful time, everything that could go wrong did.

Four months after that horrible phone call, we finally got in front of the school board. Told to be there at 6:00 p.m., we weren't heard until 11:30. Our superintendent, who I respected, and the Providence School Board, peered down on us from their dais. I was so ashamed.

The investigation had found that Buddy apparently made some nonsensical comments in class. Instead of asking a student to take a hat off his head and sit down, a student reported, "He told me to wear a chair on my head."

"I think Mr. Kenner swore at me in Russian," another student claimed. I was outraged that they considered these allegations as punishable offenses, let alone four months of agony with no dialogue.

"I got you a great deal," the school board lawyer told Buddy. "A ten-day suspension."

Buddy was always a straight shooter. I admired how he spoke to the middle school students as if they were adults. He never talked down to them. On the other hand, it is possible some at Nathan Bishop didn't appreciate his avant-garde approach or quirky sense of humor.

"I feel alone at work," he repeatedly told me in March and April. "No one ever asked for my side of the story. I don't feel valued. There's not going to be a production this spring. I just don't feel good about myself."

We went to Longboat Key for April vacation and, when we returned, the school department called again. Another allegation. Buddy had routinely asked to see a child's hall pass and it somehow made the child uncomfortable. The principal came to the auditorium and shouted down the aisle, "Pack your things, you're out of here!" Right in front of the students. No warning. No professionalism. Never privately called into the office.

It was especially difficult maintaining a positive attitude in Room 4 while agonizing over the changes. On the first day of school in 2012, after being angry for most of the 2011 school year, I took a deep breath and prayed. "Just for today, I will continue to work hard and be patient and kind with everyone I meet. And I will be open for all the life lessons I will learn from the children. Just for today." Beyond that, there was just too much to confront.

RYAN had been born at twenty-two weeks, eighteen weeks prematurely. That September was my third year with Ryan, now a fifth grader. He had two hearing aids, glasses, difficulty with speech, and mental retardation. I looked around the room as they filed out for dismissal. They were an exceptional group, attentive and eager.

"Can I get you your coat from the closet, Mrs. Kenner?" Ryan asked. He always wanted to be last in line so he could walk with me to the bus. Sometimes, he'd tell me a joke; other times, he'd hold my hand.

"Of course, Ryan. What a gentleman you are." He puffed up and flashed a crooked grin. "You did a wonderful job today! I'm looking forward to seeing you tomorrow. Tell your mom about our terrific day."

Ryan loved his mom and loved that I loved his mom. "Mrs. Kenner, can I ask you something?"

"Of course," I said.

"Are you going to be sad again tomorrow?"

"I'm sorry. What did you say?"

"Are you going to be sad again tomorrow?"

I thought I had concealed my sadness. "Maybe," I said, choosing to be honest with him. "Maybe I will be sad again tomorrow."

"Well if you are, we will help you." He took me by the hand and walked me down the hallway. "Can I ask you one more thing, Mrs. Kenner?"

"Anything, Ryan."

"Who was the roundest knight at King Arthur's round table?"

"Who?" I asked, gripping his hand with encouragement.

"Sir Cumference! Bye! See you tomorrow!" And just like that, he skipped outside. When I returned to Room 4, I sat at his desk.

Suddenly, I thought about the first time I had experienced tragedy in real time with my students. I had been pregnant with Daniel, and we were doing a unit on space that culminated with watching the launch of the Space Shuttle Challenger. The country had been united around space exploration and in the auditorium, we cheered on Christa McAuliffe, the soon-to-be first teacher in space. "How proud her parents must be," I remember thinking as the television captured her mom and dad's faces. In an instant, disaster struck. An explosion. A spider web of foamy smoke spread out into the atmosphere. Everyone gasped in horror. How do you handle tragedy in front of children?

I tried to imagine what it was like for Ryan, on the first day of a new school year, to have a teacher that was sad. A ten-year-old didn't deserve that worry. I had to get my act together. I owed it to him. If he, born with multiple strikes against him, could freely share his emotions and commitment to me, I had the responsibility to provide opportunities in school that nurtured his instincts for compassion.

I wrote and implemented a grant that paired my students with the fourth-grade class across the hall. The focus was to build tolerance and understanding for people with disabilities. Fox Point was "the little schoolhouse that could." We were one of the first two schools in Providence to be site-based managed, designing and controlling the curriculum and hiring practices to best suit our students' needs. "Learning disabilities means having average or above average intelligence but the brain has trouble processing certain areas," I told each student. Every participant went through the school day navigating and experiencing a different handicap. The conversation it stimulated had a noticeable impact on school culture and, gave all students a venue for practicing new problem-solving skills. Some kids wore earmuffs and some spent the day confined to a walker. I wanted my students to feel capable, to know that their own particular handicap wasn't an excuse. The program was a success. It helped remind me to never ask the student in a wheelchair to get up and walk across the room.

"Follow my voice," Ryan urged his peers while they tried to walk through the classroom with eye masks on. "I'll keep you safe," he said with another big grin. "Trust me. As your friend, I want to help."

"**H**ARRY was born medically fragile," his mom told me during parent teacher conferences. "Soon after he was born, my husband and I brought Harry to Boston Children's Hospital for specialized care. The doctors told us to make our peace. Say our goodbyes in case Harry couldn't come home to Providence. I went to the chapel and prayed. I thanked God. He had already answered my prayers. He had given me a son. I directed all my prayers toward the heads, hands, and hearts of those trying to save Harry's life. I will spend the rest of my life appreciative of my miracle."

My heart was reopened to how my students' pasts helped shape their present. We related, mom to mom, how to achieve acceptance in complex decisions that have to be made for family.

"I will fight for your trust," I assured Harry's mother. "I will be an extension of you. Your hopes and wishes for your son will be an upmost priority."

Later that week, I sat on the bench under the tree at recess. I couldn't help feeling anxious while Buddy was at home deciding whether to retire or be subjected to termination. I didn't know how to advise him, to protect him. I believed the system would work on his behalf and it didn't. Neither choice was right. Buddy's dream was being dragged through the mud and I couldn't help him.

I watched Harry try to traverse the monkey bars. He wasn't physically strong but he was spirited and feisty. On Monday, he had gotten across two rungs and on Tuesday he got across three. Harry kept looking over to me, not for an assist, but to make sure I was watching his progress. He hung on for dear life, the bandana around his neck absorbing the drool. He was more than halfway across. "Please, God, carry him all the way," I prayed. But then he dropped to the ground. "Darn! He didn't make it."

But his reaction was just the opposite. He got up, brushed himself off, and ran loops around the jungle gym. He didn't have a lot of words at his disposal but he was trying his best to tell his friends, "Did you see what I just did?" He was so empowered. He pumped his arms up and down like Rocky.

"I did it! I did it!"

All of a sudden, I was in the presence of God's grace. "Maybe being strong isn't holding on for dear life," I said out loud. "Maybe it's knowing when to let go." Even though Harry didn't get to the end, he had prevailed. "Oh my gosh," I realized, "it's okay for Buddy to let go." I needed to help Buddy find his Rocky move. He was a shell of the man I knew and loved and it was worsening every day. He was not going to be able to go all the way across like we had planned, to retire with the mortgage paid. But I knew for sure they were not going to fire him. That was not going to be his legacy. I decided that when I got home that night, I'd encourage him to retire with his head held high.

On September 30, 2012, with dignity intact, we went to 797 Westminster Street, listened to Buddy's name accepted for retirement and privately honored the seventeen years he worked in the Providence School Department. Though he never got to say goodbye to his students or goodbye and thank you to the families, letting go was a sign of accomplishment. Harry gave me that grace. I never looked back or had any doubt after the lesson I learned at the monkey bars.

Gingerbread Houses

On December 14, 2012, Room 4 made gingerbread houses and it felt so close to perfection. Everyone wore cheerful Christmas sweaters and Santa hats. Carols blasted and the adults got silly while the kids devoured most of the decorative candy. I cried a lot that morning, so happy to give my students a Christmas memory.

It's odd how many of life's most terrible moments are preceded by moments of lightness and joy. At lunch, a teacher came into the staff lounge with news that just ripped my heart out. A man had gone into an elementary school in Fairfield County and opened fire on the principal, teachers, and students. The little girls and boys came out of Sandy Hook Elementary with their hands over their eyes as police and first responders swarmed their school.

Many innocent people lost their lives that day, most of them six and seven years old. But Sandy Hook Elementary School was full of heroes. Several staff members, the principal included, died in order to alert the rest of the school about the intruder. Teachers and janitors barricaded doors, some even hid their students on bathroom toilets. From under her desk, the school nurse called 911.

Before Columbine, the thought of guns in schools seemed impossible. Buddy, Daniel, and I were in Washington, D.C. for April vacation when we heard how two teenage boys methodically massacred their classmates and teachers. News coverage showed kids evacuating the school with their hands up like criminals, unsure whether they had reached safety. It was unfathomable. I told Daniel, "I will always do my best to keep you safe."

He looked at me, unconvinced. "But how?"

What happened at Sandy Hook broke me. A little boy named Daniel died. There was a new normal. We were bare bones, nuts and bolts. Keeping the school stocked with paper and pencils was a daily struggle. Now we were expected to specialize in grief and mental illness. The schools were simply not prepared for such rage to permeate and divide our society. We became a generation of lockdown and intruder drills. We had simulations to safely prepare the children in case the unimaginable happened in our building, in our school. It was sickening.

What if our Christmas party was the last thing I ever got to experience? I imagined the teachers and students at Sandy Hook doing something festive. That was how I chose to think about it. I hoped they were making gingerbread houses.

The parents of Newtown were remarkable. They came together to grieve and courageously provided each other with support. I believed in staying present during tragedy, to find comfort through rituals and ceremonies. But I also learned the virtue of allowing myself to receive help, to give people the chance to be there for me.

There are moments in life that changed me, where a straight, hard line was drawn between the before and after. I had to accept that healing was a matter of stemming the damage. The effects of tragedy cannot be prevented. I didn't have that kind of control. Coping, teamwork, and tenacity: those are what the tragedies that occurred while I was a teacher, and as a wife and parent, taught me.

"This will never happen to me," was something I never said.

My Not So Funny Valentine

SAMUEL was our Boy Wonder extraordinaire. He had a seizure disorder and, as he told me, "The helmet I wear protects all the magical thoughts in my head." Every other week, Room 4 visited senior citizens at Tockwotton nursing home across the street. "The seniors sitting in," Samuel called them. Bringing children to interact with the elderly had remarkable benefits. The Tockwotton staff and residents, and the teachers and students, each took the time to get to know someone who was different and it brought out the best in each participant. The children gave them a reason to get out of their beds or rooms, which for some was a rarity. Over the course of our twenty-three-year partnership, our students discovered how to both accept and uncover their unique ways of giving to others.

The elderly also got a kick out of the simple pleasures of childhood—playing games, sharing stories and snacks, holding hands, and reading. They became peers to the children. Thrilled by a compliment after reading aloud, Samuel boasted, "You hear that, Mrs. Kenner? She says I'm a smart young man!" Ms. Adams was 104 and had experienced prejudice as one of the first black students at Pembroke College. Through stories of a past Samuel had yet to discover, she became his ally and taught him to fight against discrimination. Samuel learned to respect aging, and how to say goodbye to someone he cared about. He stood with me in a line that went around the block waiting to attend her wake.

We devoted the week before Valentine's Day in Writer's Workshop crafting keepsake cards with lacy doilies, glitter, and fancy hearts for our seniors sitting in. "Well, they're not our real grandparents," Samuel thought out loud, "and we're not their real grandchildren, but we are really friends. Can we ask them to be our grandfriends?"

～

"How is everything going?" Dr. Sanfred asked at Buddy's annual checkup.

"There are some memory and behavioral issues, excessive drinking, and talking to himself," I said, sharing some of my concerns.

Dr. Sanfred referred us to a neuropsychologist from Butler Hospital and we spent several months assessing different components of Buddy's brain functioning from planning, gross motor, fine motor, organizational skills, sequence ability, recall, and following multi-step directions. The test results were not good. There was global degeneration in all three parts of his brain. Then, an already anxiety-inducing experience took a turn for the worse; the red flag in Buddy's genetic history.

～

Buddy's mother, Roselyn, was traveling in the Bahamas with her husband and two other couples when Buddy's father, who was only fifty-three years old, suffered a fatal heart attack. Roz, a sweet woman who understood the power of a good brownie, went on vacation with the love of her life and brought him home in a coffin. Buddy was twenty at the time. His mother had to finish raising Buddy and his three brothers on her own.

There were always people who would moan and groan about their mothers-in-law but I wasn't one of them. In 2000, after Roz's eightieth birthday, she moved into an assisted living unit. She told me she was going into the bathroom to moisturize. Her skin was raw and red. Mistaking it for lotion, she reached under the sink and pulled out toilet bowl cleaner. She had been applying bleach to her birdlike skin. Though we visited many times a week, we were the last to believe she was sick. "Bud, this is serious. We need to wake up. This is not what we thought it was."

We moved her into a secured memory care unit, a circular facility, right down the block from my school. To be present for Roz's decline from Alzheimer's was a life-changing moment for all of us. Daniel, who was then a sophomore in high school, decided to compile photo albums to share with her.

"Who's that, Nan?"

"Your brother, Aaron."

"And this?"

"Your other brother. Jesse."

He pointed to a picture of himself in fifth grade. "And how about this handsome one in the wild striped shirt?"

Roz was immediately overjoyed. "Oh, that's Martin."

Daniel was crestfallen. He didn't know how to respond. I winked at him, trying to silently encourage him to keep going. "Well, it looks like Marty had a lot of fun as a fifth grader," Daniel said to her. "You must have been so proud since he was your first son."

"That was a marvelous gift," I told Daniel later. "You gave her a glimpse of Marty in fifth grade." Wherever she went in her mind, we learned to follow, improvising our way through every interaction. Though that became increasingly difficult.

After another visit, I accidentally left my water bottle inside and Daniel went back in to get it. Roz greeted him, having no memory of him just being there. The next day, Daniel said to me, "I don't want to go today."

On the next visit: "It's too hard to go."

By the third time he chose not to accompany me, I was worried it was becoming a habit. How do you be a parent in a time of heartbreak? "As long as you don't have regrets," I told him. "Regret is one of the most unproductive emotions. If you regret something, it's because it's over and done with. Wishing you had done something differently isn't going to change that. You don't want there to come a time when you say, 'If only.' If you make the decision not to go, I'm going to trust you made it for the right reasons."

Giving Daniel permission to step back, take a break, and find comfort in the fact that others were there to help allowed him the time to reflect on how he, as a teenager, could best contribute. He gave me the opportunity to learn, free from judgment, how others cope in times of crisis and helped me find my own comfort zone. He never missed another visit.

On a beautiful day, the sky full of puffy white clouds, Daniel and I walked hand-in-hand with Roz until we came to a bench by the bird feeder. "Can I sit down and rest?" she asked. Daniel stood over her, shielding her eyes from the sunlight. She looked up at him, standing tall above her, and asked, "How'd you get up so high?" I imagined she saw, all of a sudden, in the blink of an eye, her youngest grandson tall enough to reach the sky.

Eventually, Roz was assigned to a palliative care doctor. Buddy's childhood friend told us a story about his mother's last days. He had stayed by his mother's hospital bed for days and days as she was getting ready to pass. Then, the morning he snuck away to the cafeteria for a cup of coffee, she died. He was devastated. The nurse, however, explained to him that there was an art to dying. Some patients wait to be surrounded by their loved ones, but many wait to die alone in peace.

"It's all right," I whispered to Roz. "You can go to sleep. If you are fighting to stay alive for us, know that you are a great mother, a great grandmother, and an amazing mother-in-law." Roz looked at me. I don't know if she understood what I said or what I meant, but the connection we held was deep and meaningful. I brought her hand to my cheek and felt the cool band of metal against my skin. For thirty-six years she had never taken off her wedding ring.

Days later, I was in New York City with my siblings and our dad to unveil a brick at Ellis Island honoring his seventy-fifth birthday and our ancestors who had immigrated to America. We celebrated with an amazing suite at the Waldorf and center orchestra seats at the new Broadway sensation, *Wicked*. I was conflicted about where I belonged — there honoring my dad with my siblings, or with Buddy and Daniel at Roz's deathbed.

At the end of the production, the actors received a thunderous standing ovation. My phone vibrated at the exact moment I got out of my seat to clap.

A text from Daniel. *Call as soon as you can.*

I just knew. I could feel it so deeply. Roz had died.

I made my standing ovation for Roselyn Kenner.

~

In light of Roz's battle with Alzheimer's, the doctors at Butler Hospital directed us to a neurologist at The Alzheimer's Disease and Memory Disorders Center; however, Buddy's PET scan ruled out Alzheimer's.

Instead, he received the dismal diagnosis of Frontotemporal Lobe Dementia. FTD attacks the parts of the brain that deal with behavior, problem solving, emotion control and speech. "Like the preacher who starts swearing on the pulpit," was how the doctor described it. "Be prepared for aggression, a loss of empathy, dysphasia, a loss of cultural inhibitions, and an inability to do any sort of planning or organizing. He's only going to get worse. There is no cure. And as of now, there's no clinical trial. You can't be a teacher anymore," he said matter-of-factly to Buddy.

At the time, Bud was teaching one English class per semester at a local commuter college. "Oh yes I can. My students love me."

"No. You cannot be their teacher anymore. It's not fair to your students."

Buddy's shoulders slumped. "Who am I, if not a teacher?" The last bit of hope left his body like air from a balloon.

"Anything else?" asked the doctor, shooting a perfunctory glance around the room. He then stood up, closed the folder, and told us, "Sign out at the front desk." He sent us home with empty hearts and no tools or skills to help Buddy.

We left the doctor's office and went to Valentine's Day dinner on Wickenden Street. All the ladies, including me, wore pink and red. The couples looked happy, holding hands, smiling, toasting, and sipping Blackberry Sidecars.

"His brain is more like that of a seventy-five-year-old man," I remembered the doctor saying weeks earlier. I realized all of the years in between were going to pass us by. We would completely lose all of those years together. I had seen the PET scans and the MRIs. I had seen an actual X-ray of my husband's brain and had asked a million questions. Now I had to accept this new reality of what he was and wasn't capable of. I didn't want him to suffer, to feel shame, to feel unloved.

I watched Buddy in the candlelight and wondered if he ordered the Caesar salad with chicken because it was easier than choosing from a complicated menu. He stared off. I desperately wanted him to reach over, hold my hand, ask me, "What the hell just happened?" But none of that happened. That was the night, the moment, our lives disconnected. I realized exactly what I was facing and, suddenly, I couldn't stop crying.

Buddy and I met in 1979. He was a divorced father of two and the founder and owner of 3 Steeple Street Restaurant, a gathering place in Providence while the city was undergoing its urban renaissance and revitalization. My roommate was going to teach in England and asked me to take her weekend waitress shifts. Though knee-deep in the Providence School System, I was looking for a social outlet and accepted. On my first day at 3 Steeple Street, I found out the restaurant would be closed for two weeks for summer maintenance. "Why don't you start by the windows," Buddy said, handing me rubber gloves, a rag, and a bucket.

"It was love at first sight, Ro," he liked to remind me over the years. "I fell in love with you watching you wash those windows. The sunlight came right through your turquoise sundress. You looked exquisite."

He asked me out one night while I was working my section. "There's a rumor The Rolling Stones are playing Lupo's. I scored us some tickets."

"Thank you," I said, "but I can't do that to my coworkers."

Eventually, two years later, we did see The Rolling Stones to-gether. We hopped a private eight-seater and flew to Rochester; on the tarmac, we literally parked next to The Rolling Stones' jet. When they ripped through the opening chords to their new single, "Start Me Up," Mick Jagger pointed right at me in the fifth row. Buddy squeezed my hips.

"I am not able to find words big enough to tell you how much I love you. Promise me you'll never forget this night because I have never loved you more."

⌒

For more than thirty years, I was always proud to have Buddy as my husband. And it made me feel special to have a husband who returned that admiration. I was proud of the way Bud grew as a father, especially having lost his own at twenty. I made a conscious decision to help Buddy be the kind of father he wanted to be and that was a gift I gave him. To have to tell Jesse, Aaron, and Daniel that the man they idolized was no longer going to be able to be that man, be that father, broke my heart. It was devastating to think that the children had to become the men and that Buddy could no longer be their beacon. I reached for Buddy's hand across the candlelit table and slowly began to mourn the absence.

To Tickle The Goldfish

"**E**RIN is ready to fly," a colleague from Pleasant View School told me one day. "Do you have any room in your class for new students? She would do wonderfully with you. She's a dream come true. It's important for me to find a teacher who would love her as much as I do."

Born with hydrocephalus, a condition where fluid accumulates in the brain, and with parts of her frontotemporal lobe and parietal lobes missing, Erin was the epitome of resilience. I often wondered if she knew she was a child. She loved *I Love Lucy* and Wile E. Coyote cartoons. She spent recess wandering around, looking at the sky, always coming to the adults for conversation. We taught her how to play and how to talk to kids her own age.

One morning, I heard screaming from the hallway and could tell it was Erin. Still zipped in the harness she wore on the bus, she was flailing around, her wild curly hair awry. "I'm sorry, Mrs. Kenner! I'm sorry, Mrs. Kenner! Mrs. Kenner, can I please have another chance?"

"Take a breath, Erin. Slow down. What happened?"

"Please can I have another chance to think of another 'F' word to say? Can I think of another 'F' word to say? Fuck is not a good 'F' word to say on the bus anymore. Please can I think of another 'F' word?"

She would tattle on herself all the time. She would tell me what she did wrong and what the appropriate punishment should be. "What would be a good 'F' word to say?" I replied.

"Well, I will say 'Friendship'…'Family'…'Flowers'…'French fries.' Please can I have another chance to say another 'F' word?"

It was hard to get mad at her.

During breakfast that day, the kids were served microwaved poached eggs in a bag. Erin set up her desk like a five-star dining experience. "Well, this certainly looks like it's going to be an eggs-traordinary day," she announced, wiggling her little arms like a chicken. "Everyone eggs-cited about their breakfast?"

I played along. "Erin, that is eggs-cellent! You are eggs-ceptionally brilliant! Go across the hall and tell Mrs. Martin and Room 7 how eggs-uberant you are."

Forty-five minutes later she came back with a notebook containing two columns of words that began with "Eggs." My assistant and I cried from laughing so hard. Erin came to my desk, took me by the hand, and said, "Mrs. Kenner, your laughter is getting eggs-tremely annoying. Go over to the quiet chair and think about your life choices."

As I sat in timeout, soon to be known as the "think about your life choices chair," I realized I hadn't laughed since Valentine's Day. I had felt so sorry for myself, tired from agonizing over my life and Buddy's problems. Still laughing, I said to the class, "Justice is a virtue and justice has been eggs-trajudicially been served."

"Mrs. Kenner," Erin asked preciously, "what's a virtue?"

"Virtues are important qualities that help make you a good person. Being trustworthy and honest, having courage, being patient."

"Oh, I'm good at those!" she rejoiced. "Remember the time my dad asked who spilled the water all over the rug and I told him I was just trying to tickle the goldfish?"

And just like that, my heart rejoiced. I was comfortable pausing, leaning into the unknown to make room for small miracles every day. Erin once asked me if I would ever forget being her teacher. Never in a million years. She made me believe in the potential of the human brain when Buddy received his depressing prognosis and helped me understand how people communicate in spite of the odds.

Downhill

The principals and the teachers and the kids usually get all the accolades, but everyone really knows it is the staff in the main office and the custodians who run a school. Mrs. Stone and Mrs. Fuller were administrative assistants, but visitors assumed they were assistant principals. Mrs. Stone was the right-hand woman to many principals and one of the longest-tenured employees in the Providence School System. She was very proud of the students—the girls particularly—and never saw them as handicapped. Always the first person to give a generous donation, she started the Coffee Brigade with Amos House homeless shelter. "Let's do it in January and February when people have forgotten to donate." She retired due to illness after working fifty-plus years. On her deathbed, she held her hand out to me and asked me to carry on the school's legacy.

Mrs. Fuller was her sidekick and something like the school mascot. She wore Fox Point clothes everywhere, organized dress-down days for charities, and helped run the food drives. The more difficult the student, the easier it was for Mrs. Fuller to get through to them. We went through many, many hard times together.

That week after Valentine's Day, I checked my voicemail before sitting down with our family lawyer who specialized in elder law. It was from a former student who shared the amazing news that he had graduated college, where he'd studied to become a library specialist. "Mrs. Kenner, I just visited our school and Mrs. Fuller gave me your phone number. I hope you're not mad. She told me you were having a hard time and that Mr. Kenner is sick. I want you to know I appreciate the way you were there for me when I was going through a difficult time. And now I want to be there for you when you're having a difficult time."

After I signed the complex legal documents, our lawyer said, "Maureen, I'm going to be very honest: in my experience, when a couple is as close and devoted to each other as you and Buddy, when something happens to one, the other can go downhill."

I sat at the dining room table in silence, stunned.

O-Positive

ARIANNA had voiced her concern that on the long hot days after the September 11 terrorist attacks, the firefighters must've gotten really thirsty. "How about we collect quarters for water to send to the firefighters?"

"You are so smart! That sounds like an excellent way to help," I told her. I left school that day proud to be in the company of children, once again, during a time of tragedy. Our family had lost two cousins, one in each of the Twin Towers, each just starting their lives. Like every American, I felt helpless. What could I do to help my family, my community, my country?

I decided, as blood type O-positive, I would donate blood to those in need. I established the ritual of going to the Rhode Island Blood Center every few months on Saturday mornings with a good book and the chance to reflect on the importance of watching others serve the greater good. The staff at the blood center was always kind and complimentary. They gave me extra snacks for my students and enjoyed hearing stories from the classroom. I'd think about my dad and brother Michael, scrambling out of New York City on the morning of 9/11. I'd think about all the first responders, men, women and children, so many from the Rockaway Beach neighborhood, who were forever changed that day.

I thought of Arianna again during my 2013 physical when Dr. Sanfred asked, "Is there anything else I can help you with today?" We had spent most of the appointment talking about Buddy, dementia, and ways to help me manage the stress. Buddy, once vibrant and articulate, was now quiet. The blessing was once he got the FTD diagnosis and understood he had a disease in his brain, there was no more aggression. He became content, experiencing and expressing more joy. But my partner, my spouse, my lover, my friend, my rabble-rouser was quickly vanishing and new roles were emerging. I had given care as a daughter and a sister and a mom; those roles came naturally. But I was hesitant reminding a grown man to shower, to get dressed, to chew, to swallow his food, to come to bed.

"Well," I told Dr. Sanfred, "I've been a regular blood donor since September 11, but I've been deferred for low iron the past three attempts. I feel disappointed I can't donate."

The fluorescent lights in the examination room flickered in rhythm with the hum of the air conditioner. The table was cold against my legs. I shivered, clenching the johnny gown. Usually by July I was already tan but I had spent the first three weeks of summer vacation indoors trying to dig out from the collateral damage that erupted with Buddy's early onset dementia. Dementia wreaked havoc on our life; every day was spent on the phone and the computer trying to untangle our unpaid taxes and mortgage. If everything else was going to diminish — our conversations, our memories, our lives — and if he was going to become disoriented, I wanted Buddy to be around his familiar things: his home and neighborhood we both loved.

"On the way out, I'll order you a complete blood panel. Not a problem," Dr. Sanfred said.

~

From our home office, I looked out the window and saw Buddy on the lounge, enjoying the summer heat out in the yard, staring off, watching the clouds take shape. Unable to get into summer mode, I stayed busy trying to find a clinical trial for him, trying to figure out the next step in a life spinning out of control. I was preoccupied on the computer when the phone rang. Buddy was beginning to become uncomfortable answering the phone and I was irritated by those seemingly little changes. I picked up the phone and awkwardly cupped it between my ear and my shoulder, my neck twisted and tense.

"Maureen, it's David Sanfred. I have your blood tests back. They show high levels of anemia. I want you to see a specialist."

The Citibank webpage glared at me. My face was hot from the sunlight coming through the blinds. I watched Buddy smile as a blue jay splashed around the birdbath. "I'm sorry. Who is this?"

"It's David Sanfred. Your blood levels show alarming levels of anemia. For women age fifty-plus, this can be a sign of colon cancer."

"I'm sorry. You have the wrong number!" I said, annoyed.

"Maureen, you sound distracted. You need to stop what you're doing and listen to what I'm saying. It's very serious. I'm going to call a doctor. A specialist. I want you to go see him. I'll make the appointment for next Monday."

The phone was too heavy and it dropped onto the keyboard. I watched all the work I had done on the Citibank webpage disappear.

No Longer My Person

GERRY was a petite, hyperactive baseball player who was never quite comfortable in his own skin. One day, he began to pull out his hair. "Help me understand," I urged him. "Tell me what you are feeling."

"Well, I feel like I'm at the mall at Christmas," he articulated.

The night before my colonoscopy, I completely knew how he felt. It was Monday night. *The Bachelorette* was on. Desiree was getting ready to choose her beau. I kept the volume high so I didn't miss her decision while frantically running in and out of the bathroom. The colonoscopy was scheduled for 8:00 the next morning. I was agitated and overloaded but there was no time to back out. I had no symptoms, no family history, but at fifty-five I had never had a colonoscopy. Every year since I turned fifty, I'd scheduled one per the doctor's orders. I even bought the laxatives and stool softener to prep but, every year, I'd canceled. That decision would soon haunt me.

Buddy went with me to the colonoscopy. I gave him my notebook and pen, told him to be ready to take notes after it was over. Notes about the iron pills or the iron-rich diet I'd probably need, notes about the follow-up blood work. The nurse led me in to the prep room, cold and fluorescent just like the last one, and left me to put on another blue johnny. She reminded me of our daughter-in-law, a doctor in Virginia, so I felt comfortable as she wheeled me in to the procedure. In my head, I had built it up to be awful, but, as I dozed off to Vivaldi in that dark cobalt room, a strong sense of peace came over me. The same dark cobalt, I noticed, as the dining room at 3 Steeple Street Restaurant.

I woke up in the recovery room with Buddy at the left side of my bed. The doctor stood over me. The nurse at the foot of my bed asked if I wanted anything to drink. My voice cracked, dehydrated. "How about orangeade?" My mom used to make that on hot summer days. Orange juice and ice water stirred with a bit of sugar.

"I'm sorry to tell you this, but we found some cancer," the doctor said. "It has to come out right away. I'm sorry."

All I heard was, "WHAH WHAH WHAH," in thought bubbles over my head. I felt like Charlie Brown. The drugs must have been wearing off. "I'd really like that orangeade." The nurse's eyes were weepy above her mask.

"You need to listen to me," the doctor said. "This is very serious. We found some cancer. It needs to come out."

I looked to Buddy, seeking some kind of sympathetic understanding from him, hoping he'd clear up the confusion. On his lap, the notebook was closed and the pen was nowhere to be found. He stared at me, unable to offer anything. He simply couldn't.

"Who is your next of kin?" the doctor asked. "Who is your Power of Attorney?"

It was one of the saddest days of my marriage. I knew then that Buddy was no longer my person, that he could not help me, advocate for me, ask questions for me, comfort me. Buddy would have been with me every step of the way if he hadn't been robbed by FTD. He would have been a problem solver, he would have known how to organize projects, how to find the right people to help, how to rally the community, how to make plans to distract me. He would have done the shopping, the cooking, paid the bills. He would have brought me flowers and held my hand. He would have talked to me, listened, let me cry. He would have let me yell and scream and be scared. He would have known and cared if I left the room, left the house. He would have been there for me, completely.

WINTER

I Have Cancer

I lay on my bed shielding my swollen eyes from the sun. Buddy was out in the yard, reading. I needed to find a surgeon to remove the cancer from my colon. It had only been four months since Buddy's diagnosis. I had too many responsibilities to be sick. How could I be the wife and mother, daughter and sister, mentor and friend I needed to be?

I called Dr. Sanfred. "If it were your wife or your daughter, what surgeon would you recommend?"

"Dr. Sahni Minhas. He's the best. I would take my wife or my daughter to Dr. Minhas. I *have* taken my mother to Dr. Minhas. I've already called to tell him I have somebody special I need taken care of."

How would I start talking about cancer? How would I even say it? *I have cancer.* I hadn't said it aloud yet.

"I have cancer," I kept repeating in my mind, waiting for the words to change.

How would I tell my family? Once I told others, cancer would be my reality. I looked at the clock. My mom would be at the Ardsley Swim Club, swimming laps, or sitting where the sun warmed the white walls under the clock. I couldn't bring myself to pick up the phone, ruin her day.

"Everything will change once I make this call," I thought.

I couldn't bring myself to call anyone, not Daniel, my sisters, my brothers, or my dad. I could not pick up the phone.

I wondered what it would feel like to simply walk outside, sit on the lounge chair next to Bud, watch the birds plunge

45

into the birdbath, and think about what was for dinner. Or think about getting the clothes out of the dryer. Or about what to pack for our upcoming trip to Martha's Vineyard with our grandchildren. I was too busy planning my life to think about cancer or surgeons.

The phone by our bed rang. And rang. I let the answering machine pick up.

It was Dr. Minhas's office calling about my appointment in three days.

∿

I joined Buddy for a walk. "I'm worried!" I sobbed, feeling frazzled and lost in my own neighborhood. "They said I have cancer!" It was the first time I said it aloud and it rushed out like a riptide. I leaned against a picket fence, coughing and dizzy, afraid I was going to collapse from despair. But Buddy, focused on the traffic at the crosswalk ahead, didn't respond. "Bud, please! I'm telling you I'm scared!" I grabbed for his hand in his blue fleece.

"I don't know what to say." This was the apathy his doctor had warned about.

"How do you not know what to say?" I pleaded.

A lady walking her Jack Russell Terrier stopped and stared. "Go along with your business," I cried out to her. "I have cancer and my husband's not responding. I'm allowed to be angry!"

Buddy spoke softly, but it wasn't clear to whom he was talking.

"There you go. Good boy."

∿

My mom and my sister Dianne came with me to meet Dr. Minhas, while Daniel stayed with Buddy in the waiting area. Another freezing cold examination room. More waiting, waiting, and waiting. Dr. Minhas posted the scans for us to see and confirmed it was cancer. "I believe it is Stage 1 because of the location, the lack of symptoms, your age, and your overall good health."

Everything happened so fast. Dianne feverishly scribbled notes as Dr. Minhas spoke, interjecting to ask questions and hurrying to record the answers. I sat there shivering, wrapping the paper from the examining table around my legs. "I don't have time for this," I thought.

"Get this out of your body and off your mind," Dr. Minhas said.

At the desk, we scheduled the surgery for July 29, 2013. The three of us walked out to the lobby. We held hands, leaned into each other, and cried. Buddy stood up. Daniel approached, hesitant, cautious. The room spun. "It's serious," I told Daniel. He looked around the waiting room and then hushed me.

"Mom, you're scaring the rest of these patients!"

He corralled our family into a huddle. I thought about the end of the *Mary Tyler Moore Show* in the newsroom with Mary and Lou Grant and Ted Baxter. I needed a tissue so, clumped together, we plodded over to the tissue box. Heads bowed, clinging to each other, we made our way to the elevator. As we stepped in, together as a team, Daniel said, "Well, this calls for a root beer float!"

LYSANDER was one of only a handful of students over the years I was nervous about having in Room 4. He was a big tough bully with Down syndrome. "Dear Lord," I thought, "how am I going to do this? How will he interact with the other kids?"

We had remarkably few accidents and injuries for an elementary school, but one afternoon an episode of roughhousing resulted in a boy being pushed through a plate glass window in the hallway outside the courtyard, opening a deep wound on his head. There was blood like I had never seen. An aide ran out from the cafeteria, took off her sweatshirt, and made a tourniquet around the gash.

"Get all my kids out of the hallway!" Mrs. Martin yelled to me. I waved the kids into Room 4.

"Boys and girls," I told my students, "quickly make room for our friends from Room 7. We have company." Whenever I said, "We have company," my kids knew to get into gear, make room, use their manners and offer help. Many of the Room 7 kids cried, shaken up by the bleeding and screaming. Lysander passed around tissues and Beanie Babies, and offered his Writer's Notebook and crayons in case kids wanted to color. Then he went to the sink, filled up other people's water bottles and brought over oranges and bananas. "Youse have to share. We don't have enough for all of youse, so youse have to share."

I witnessed the beauty of community that had arisen from crisis. Room 7's children were friends my kids rode the bus with, ate in the cafeteria with, and had recess with. And now, when they needed us, my kids knew that when in doubt, give them tissues, tools to be creative, water, and food. I thought I had to be strong and reassuring because we didn't know the severity of the injury, but the kids, especially Lysander, did all of the nurturing. I was honored to be with them when they read a chapter, accomplished a math problem, nurtured a seed, discovered an interest, or performed in a production, but the way they helped one another reassured me that sometimes the world seemed a little less scary through the eyes of a child. Even though we had the routine of the classroom, we welcomed each day with wonderment and curiosity and, in this way, we found grace in the situations that called upon us to act.

I began to feel like I would let my students down, that my illness would neglect their learning. The 2012-2013 school year in Room 4 had been one of the happiest, with many of the best students and staff working together. I looked forward to having many of the same students again in the fall as fifth graders. I wanted them to feel smart, to feel free to imagine their future so I had already started to plan the first few back-to-school units for my young writers, readers, geologists, paleontologists, botanists, mathematicians, and electricians. I had signed up for a two-week summer professional development adventure with Save the Bay, a local preservation society. Professional development activities always exhilarated me because I brought back such exciting hands-on learning opportunities for my students. I pictured the budding scientists in Room 4 gathered around a tank full of crustaceans with enthusiasm, each absorbing its lessons at their own pace, in their own unique way.

But as surgery got closer, I had to cancel the professional development as well as our family vacations to Martha's Vineyard and Cape Cod. My role as teacher was put on hold. I had to learn how to be a person with cancer. Upon hearing about my cancer, a colleague helped me transform my pre-surgery work into SMART goals, like those we wrote for the kids and the district: Specific, Measurable, Achievable, Results-focused, and Time-bound. She redirected my attention to focus on what I *could* manage, instead of what terrified me.

I got tired talking about cancer and dementia over and over again when, coincidentally, my daughter-in-law introduced us to CaringBridge.org. Designed to keep family and friends updated without having to talk on the phone for hours, it was a place for me to tell our story, to keep the information flowing, to ask for help.

On July 29, 2013, I was admitted to Miriam Hospital in Providence for surgery to remove the cancer in my colon. "Plan for a recuperation of seven days," Dr. Minhas told me. As I packed, I thought of my years as an assistant coach at Special Olympics. The kids competed with exhilaration and literally flew across the track. Never once did I hear a Special Olympian complain it was too hard. Their motto was "Let me win, but if I cannot win, let me be brave in my attempt." Their attempts were heroic. So, I packed the items that helped make me comfortable—just the ba-sics—as if I were going on a mini retreat: new Carole Hochman pjs, Philosophy skin care products, a floral pillowcase that used to be my grandmother's, and the Dammit! Doll my nephew David had sent me. I said "Dammit" a lot those days.

The Power Of Parents

Dianne stood by the gurney as Mom led us in prayer. I reminded Dr. Minhas about the new hard lump I felt in my belly button, something he assured me could later be handled by a dermatologist. "But, we'll give it a look," he said as he drew a circle around my belly button with a black sharpie.

Doctors and nurses in blue scrubs hustled, shuffling their feet as they prepared for my procedure. It was like being in Santa's workshop, elves milling about fastidiously, laying out their tools, objects passing hands in a blur as buttons were pressed and IV levels adjusted. I felt like a trespasser. Amidst the preparations, they chatted.

"Where's a good place to bring my in-laws for dinner?" asked one nurse through his blue face mask. Another was attending a baby shower later that day; she'd made brownies.

I recognized Dr. Minhas' gentle brown eyes.

"We are ready to go. You are in good hands."

~

After a three-hour surgery and two-hour recovery, I was wheeled into a hospital suite filled to the brim with flowers. Eager for a progress report, I said, "How did I do? How did the surgery go?" My voice sounded like it belonged to someone else.

"Would you please stop asking the same questions over and over again?" the nurse said. She put me in a post-op time out. I decided to focus only on the jobs I had to do to recover. One day at a time. I would let the pathology information filter down to me from the doctors. Feeling out of control, I intentionally took control and didn't ask again.

I detected a strain around me. Buddy sat in the corner, gazing. The despairing realization that he would not be able to help overwhelmed the family. My mom and Daniel cried.

～

The doctors warned the first and second days would be the hardest and that proved to be true. My mom stayed in the chair by my bed that first night whispering softly to me as I fought off nightmares. I remembered those Friday nights in high school when I'd sneak off to Ferncliff Cemetery for Boones Farm and Tareyton cigarettes and my sisters would cover for me over and over again.

"I'm sorry I didn't call you when I was late," I said to my mom from my hospital bed. "I know you were scared when I didn't keep my promises. I shouldn't have ignored you."

She put a cool compress on my forehead. "I'm just so glad to be here for you when you need me. You have been so strong. I am so proud of you." In a daze, I thought about the night Riley's mom sat at her daughter's desk in Room 4, looking through her daughter's workbook. "Who did this writing?" she had asked. When I answered, a big tear dropped down her cheek. "My Riley did this? I've never seen her do anything like this. Her teacher last year told me she never wrote in a notebook, she sat in the corner tearing paper all day. I've never seen something so beautiful."

～

Night two, Daniel stayed in the chair beside my bed. We talked at length about Buddy's best friend, Robert Handwerger, and the time we spent in Florida as Robert was dying. Robert was a fifth son to Roz, and his mom Shirley was a second mother to Buddy. They were three years old when spunky little Buddy approached Robert outside of his house on Stadium Road. Buddy and Robert became brothers. They were always a part of each other's lives. Robert was Buddy's best man at our wedding. He made me feel like the best spouse for his best friend. "You married up," he told Buddy. "Ro is the best thing to happen to you."

It was horrible for Buddy to see his best friend, his brother so full of light, begin to be snuffed out. The specialists spent a month ruling out a laundry list of neurological ailments, only to settle on a diagnosis of CJD, Creutzfeldt-Jakob's Disease. His prognosis was six months to a year. Everyone always told Robert, "You're one in a million." That wasn't what they meant.

"How did you feel near the end?" Daniel asked.

"At the end of our last visit, an hour before we had to leave, I wanted some time alone with Robert. He was bedridden, on hospice, not moving much throughout the day, but he was at peace and seemed comfortable. I watched him lie still, his eyes motionless and dormant. Then, we heard Buddy laughing from the kitchen. Suddenly, Robert's eyes came alive. Into focus."

"Yeah, I remember this," Daniel said. "Robert said, 'That's Buddy. Buddy's here.'"

"That's right. He recognized Dad's laugh. I leaned in and said, 'I love you. Thank you for being such a good friend to Buddy. Thank you for always telling him he got it right when he married me. Don't be afraid.'"

The Handwerger family held Robert's funeral back in Rhode

Island. We hosted the luncheon after the service, at which Buddy gave a radiant eulogy. In the yard, Shirley, who had just buried her son, took her first peaceful nap in ten months. We all laughed and had Caserta's Pizzeria and drank beer and scarfed down divine desserts. At the dining room table, a man scooped heaps of food onto his plate. "How did you know the deceased?" he asked.

"He was my husband's best friend," I said. "How did you know Robert?"

"Oh, I didn't. I saw all the cars and thought this was an open house." He helped himself to a few more pieces of pastrami, went to the living room and sat down. On a day to celebrate Robert, we already had so many opportunities to laugh, and then a man crashed his funeral. Robert would have welcomed him with open arms.

"No one wanted the day to be over," I reminded Daniel. "It felt more like a great wedding than a funeral. Some people went up to Federal Hill, where Robert had renovated and revitalized the Pastiche building, and brought back carrot cake and chocolate mousse. The lightning bugs were out but no one wanted to leave." I took Daniel by the hand. "Thank you for staying with me tonight. Coming together in times of grief is better than pulling apart. The harder things get, the harder it'll be to remember that."

"I'll be here every step of the way. I wouldn't have it any other way. How about some more ice to sooth your throat, Mom?"

I awoke later in a drug-induced fog. "Call my brother John. Tell him I'm homesick here at camp. I want my parents to pick me up."

Daniel tiptoed, like the Grinch who stole Christmas, past the end of my bed, laptop in hand.

"What time is it?" I asked.

"It's midnight, Mom. Go back to sleep."

"Where are you going?"

"They have free Wi-Fi. I'm going to do a mock fantasy football draft."

"You offered to spend the night with me in the hospital for the free Wi-Fi?" I giggled, amused by his ability to distract himself. I pushed Daniel to work hard like I pushed my students. "Maureen gets her kids a college-level education in an elementary school setting," I heard on more than one occasion. That wasn't to say Room 4 didn't make time for "Free Time Fridays" or "Gum and Games." I wanted the students to know hard work paid off. That it was okay to schedule relaxation and fun. I wanted to give them a chance to gravitate toward new hobbies. I wanted to see who wanted to do arts and crafts, who wanted to brush the doll's hair for a tea party, who wanted to play Connect 4, who wanted to work on the computer, who wanted to read, who wanted to clean, who wanted to water the plants or feed the crayfish.

On Day 3, I awoke at 5:00 a.m. Daniel was looking right at me, holding my hand, smiling. "You made it, Mom."

"*We* made it, Dan."

"We made it, Mom."

As planned, Dr. Minhas removed the tumor from the right side of my colon. Unfortunately, the hard lump under my belly button was another malignant growth. They got it out successfully, but by removing my belly button, my post-retirement job as a belly dancer was now caput.

I had such a passion for being in the classroom with my special students, families, and colleagues but Dr. Sanfred had just told me

I couldn't do that job. If not a teacher, then what? Where would I channel my passions? Find my fulfillments? I had an immediate identity crisis. Mary Poppins had gone home for the day when Dr. Minhas came into my room, 379 North, and realized I was crying.

"Sweetie. What's the matter? What is it?"

"If only I had done the colonoscopy, none of this would have happened."

Dr. Minhas sat down and took me by the hand. "I'm going to tell you a story. Then I don't want to talk about it again. Now listen carefully. My father was coming to Rhode Island from Pakistan. He told all of his friends he was going to visit his son, 'the surgeon in Rhode Island. The Ocean State.' All he wanted to do when he got to Rhode Island was to go fishing with me. That was our thing when I was a little boy. Fishing. So, my dad came to Rhode Island. But then he got sick. And the days got busy. I never got to go fishing with my dad. The one thing he wanted, I was never able to give him. He passed away. For months and months, I beat myself up over it. I was so sad, so heartbroken to know I would never again go fishing with my dad. I would never get that chance." Dr. Minhas put my hand to his heart. "You can never go back," he said slowly. "Do not spend a moment of your time trying to change the past because you're going to sabotage your healing. You need to put that behind you and focus on the present and on the future."

A lightness came over me. I was confident I could follow his advice. He gave me the greatest gift of my healing in the hospital. No longer did I have any guilt. People prepared me to be angry at "Mr. Cancer." Angry with God. Angry with myself. Angry with my physicians for not picking up on it. But I was no longer angry. For that moment, I was released.

Orientation Vs. Oncology

On August 27, 2013, still recuperating, I made the first visit to my oncologist, Dr. Robert Mandel, at Miriam Hospital Fain 3 Cancer Center. It was the same day as Fox Point's school orientation. A day meant to reunite and reconnect. The unfair irony of how I spent the day didn't escape me. "You are the best person for Room 4," my mom said, "but for the moment, the substitute is the right person." I prayed I had the willpower to get oriented inside a world with cancer.

"I can take the next person," the receptionist said, coaxing me to her window to check in. "Is that you, miss?"

I couldn't move my feet.

"Over here, please," she said. I walked to the second window. I fidgeted with my fleece, took out my health card and checkbook from my purse, and grabbed the Purell to scrub my hands. Waiting for my mom to join me, I locked back. A patient with a bright pink bandanna on her head pointed to the hanging TV screen. "Does anyone else find it uncomfortable having to watch a hair loss commercial in a cancer center?" She chuckled. My mom was sitting next to her. "There's a hair loss commercial in a cancer center. Doesn't anyone find that insensitive?"

Nobody laughed.

The soap opera resumed. A priest leaned over the bedside of a perfectly coiffed female patient making the sign of the cross.

"Okay, this is just too much! Doesn't anyone find it uncomfortable to watch a priest giving last rites in a cancer center?" She was trying to rally us together like Enjolras to the students of the June Rebellion after the death of General Lamarque in *Les Misérables*. "No one?"

"Mom, come on," I urged. "It's our turn. You're with me." It was typical of my mom to gravitate towards people who needed help. I watched her sit there, holding that beautiful woman's hand, having already learned she was thirty-two years old with breast cancer and receiving her third round of chemotherapy with two toddlers at home.

"Mom, we're not here to make friends," I called across the room. "We're here to listen to what they have to say. We're not going to be here long."

$$\sim$$

A dear friend knew Dr. Mandel from her days in radiation oncology at Rhode Island Hospital. He had a reputation as a fighter. I told him I was a Special Ed teacher and asked him to make me his homework. He told me about his life, about traveling to international conferences, working on the plane through the night, creating teams of scientists serving patients around the world. "We're going to try and find you the right chemo combination because we need to get you well!"

Good teachers and good students come to learn that important work cannot be accomplished alone. My mom always said, "The more people who love my children, the better." Just as my students in Room 4 received help from a full-time teacher's assistant, speech therapists, occupational and physical therapists, guidance counselors, and social workers, Dr. Mandel assigned me to a Miriam Hospital Fain 3 team with a teaching nurse, nutritionist, and nurse navigator. Each of them presented me with another binder. Teachers often joke, "Beware another binder!" I had binders for learning about cancer, chemotherapy, nausea, diarrhea, dizziness, insomnia, weight loss, and loss of appetite. Loss and more loss. I highlighted the sections I thought might be useful later.

Slowly I found myself looking for the gains instead of the losses. I signed up for all the complementary services to improve my physical, spiritual, emotional, and mental health — massages and Yoga Nidra, acupuncture, Reiki, and Live Strong classes at the Eastside YMCA. By doing so, I recalled the time Principal Angeline Brooks phoned me in Room 4. "There are three students here from the Howard Swearer Center for Public Service at Brown University. They have an idea for a project that has your name written all over it." They wanted to pair children with learning disabilities with college mentors who had similar disabilities. Their motto was "You are not alone, and you can do this." I could tell they were on to something special. All they needed was someone to give them a chance. Their program, Eye to Eye, empowered my children to imagine following in another's footsteps and gave college students a chance to redo uncomfortable parts of their childhood. So, in preparation for chemotherapy, I followed Fox Point's model and said "Yes!" to each and every opportunity the hospital presented to me in an attempt to try to unlock the piece of the puzzle that would bring me closer to the life I wanted.

Hope

LEAH AND COURTNEY were sisters I'd taught long ago. The night before Chemo #1, Leah called out of the blue. She had heard from Mrs. Fuller that I would be home undergoing chemotherapy. "If anyone can do it, Mrs. Kenner, you can. I have faith in you. I can pray for you. I want you to know the lessons you taught me made a difference. I still argue with Courtney that you were my teacher first!" Leah had been a good student; she'd put one-hundred-percent effort into everything she did. She had been very proud of our school and always showed off Room 4 to her family.

Courtney lit up Room 4. She came to school every day with her hair styled, lips glossed, outfits patterned, and with fully-accessorized, colorful jewelry to match. She took pride in herself, her work, and her friendships and relationships, both at home and in school. During her time at school, there was a school-wide project in which the students went out into the Fox Point neighborhood to observe life, interview the locals, and use those experiences to write original stories and plays. Courtney asked to be one of the interviewers, a very important and demanding job. She struggled with reading out loud, but the people of the neighborhood were patient and kind as she went through her list of prepared questions. The project helped her develop the confidence to speak in a group and earned the respect of everyone involved.

I heard some scuffling from the other side of the phone and

then giggling. "Mrs. Kenner! It's me, Courtney! Guess what? I'm going to apply to RISD to become a fashion designer!"

"Stay strong," Leah encouraged in the background.

I heard that phrase a lot in the next few weeks. Strong enough to take on the chemotherapies, strong enough to help my family, strong enough to be the person they expected me to be, the person I wanted to be. It was a pretty tough request.

From where do we get our strength? On Shore Path in Bar Harbor, Maine, there is a boulder, tipped up against another, formed from a glacier during the Ice Age. It has lain there for ten thousand years. The tides come in and go out, pounding its surfaces, and yet there it lays, perfectly stable, balanced. Is it possible to be strong and weak at the same time?

Chemo #1—a day I feared—brought the chance to see first-hand the presence of positivity. Friends from Buddy's Early Stage Dementia Support Group delivered a cozy pink fleece blanket with matching bedazzled slippers, ginger teas and candies, music, books, and, knowing how I missed the fun school supplies, my very own coloring book and sharpened color pencils!

Rhode Island's motto is one word: "Hope." Through the day, I reflected on the question "Where do I find my hope?"

My first nurse in Radiology was, like me, the second of five children. She was also the cousin of my Special Education Director. "You will always be a Special Ed teacher but, for this quarter, you are a student of science."

A tall, dark and handsome physician's assistant inserted the port into my chest. He shared that his own mother, a Special Ed teacher of thirty-plus years, was completing her very last cancer treatment. Her hospital was directly across from my nephew David's freshman dorm at the University of Pittsburgh.

I was not the patient who was able to "make friends with the port." It gave me the creeps. Friends who had chemo told me to imagine the medicine as a "golden light" working its magic through my body. I couldn't do it. I tried meditation and visualizations but simply couldn't imagine it as golden or as light. It was poisonous, toxic, and heavy, like lead was being pumped through my body. I had to coach myself into thinking I was going to the spa. First stop: massage. Second stop: "juice bar" with Maye, my chemotherapy nurse.

"Ready?" she asked. "On the count of three. One... two... three. Deep breath."

I cried as the needle pierced my skin. Maye had also taken care of a friend of mine who'd lost her battle to cancer. "Her wife still sends flowers every year on the first day of spring to thank the staff," she told me. I could not imagine what it was like for Maye to spend her days watching patients fend off death.

It took hours for the full battery of chemotherapies—Oxaliplatin, Leucovorian and "my favorite," Fluorouracil—to be administered. Then, my IV course beeped and flashed "INFUSION COMPLETE PRESS STOP."

Maye stopped me as I was taking off my wool chemo socks, ready to leave. "I told you about my daughter earlier. Would you like to see a picture?" she asked. "I can't help myself. She just turned one."

Where would I find hope? In the heads, hands, and hearts of those around me. "Of course, I'd like to see," I said. "Don't be silly."

She opened her phone and showed me a fat-cheeked baby girl lying on her belly, propped up on her pudgy forearms. "She's so precious," I said, feeling woozy. "What's her name?"

"Her name is Hope."

The Hill

THOMAS, one of my very first handicapped students, had Cerebral palsy and spent his life in a wheelchair. He thought I was the biggest nag for not letting him only read about Boston sports teams. One day, he got so frustrated at me that he gave me the finger. His little finger shook as he struggled to keep it up. Rage flooded my body. My first thought was, "You are in big trouble, mister!" Then something came over me. "Good for you," I told Thomas. "You have so many limitations. You are letting me know how you feel." Deep down he was a fighter.

It was the morning after Chemo #2 and all I wanted was to go back to sleep. Buddy was standing at the bureau wearing black boxers and a light blue Bob Dylan T-shirt. He put his watch on his left arm and the identification wristband he wore in case of emergency on his right. The fact that I was no longer in school helped him continue to do as well as he was; I got to see the new normal, learn it, prepare for it, and set it up the way he needed. "Bud, think about taking a shower. Take off the wristband before you get in." I should have gotten up to offer help but my body wouldn't let me. The days immediately after chemo felt like a heartbreak hill on the last mile of a marathon.

When I was finally out of bed, there was no sign of him. Not in the bathroom, not at the dining room table, not on the couch; the newspaper was in, so he had already been out to the yard. I panicked. I put on my bathrobe and drove up and down Elmgrove

Avenue, weaving onto the side streets looking for a man with wild hair in black boxers. On the #40 public bus that drove by was an advertisement for Miriam Hospital: *Extraordinary care to bring your life back to ordinary.*

Finally, I spotted Buddy, in a light fall windbreaker, stretching his calves on a fire hydrant. Once he recognized the car, he smiled crookedly. He wasn't wearing his wristband, probably because I told him to take it off for the shower, the shower that never happened. Buddy was a runner, three hundred and sixty-five days a year, and luckily enough, his boxers looked like running shorts.

"You left the house without telling me!" I yelled. "I thought you were getting ready for your Silver Sneakers class at the Y."

"I felt like getting a cookie."

"You can't just leave without letting me know where you're going!"

"I didn't know I needed…I didn't know I needed…I didn't know I needed a permission slip. Next time I go somewhere, I'll get you to sign a permission slip." I couldn't help seeing a flash of the Buddy I'd fallen in love with. Suddenly, I thought of Thomas flipping me the bird.

"No, honey," I assured Buddy. "You're retired. You don't need a permission slip to go get a chocolate chip cookie." A recent Alzheimer's and Dementia Caregiver's Conference taught me it was important for the afflicted to retain their freedom and their pride. Unintentionally, I had humiliated him, taken away what the presenters called his "Peacock Moment."

As I drove home, I worried that neither of us would be strong enough to keep our vows. I had such a strong sense of accomplishment for all Buddy and I had achieved together, but it was clear to me that our happiest days may have been behind us.

I thought back to the time in the early nineties after Buddy and I had gone to see *Pulp Fiction.* I thought it was the most horrifying, disgusting movie I had ever seen and I couldn't get the foaming-at-the-mouth overdose scene out of my head. Buddy had a completely different take. "No, no. It was a dark comedy. It was a dark comedy," he said as we drove home from the theater. I had screamed for him to pull the car over.

"If you really think that, we are not cut out for each other!" I just didn't get it. What he had liked were the same scenes that repulsed me. "How are we going to make it through big decisions if we can't even agree this was a horrendous, crappy movie?"

"Years from now," he had said laughing hysterically, "when people ask why our marriage broke up, we're going to have to say *Pulp Fiction.*"

Buddy hadn't realized I had gone to Chemo #5. When I came back, he didn't ask how the day went. Didn't ask how I felt. The eyes that used to light up when I walked into a room became more and more blank. He was on the living room couch, rereading the same page of a Lee Child mystery he'd been reading the night before.

We bundled up and took a walk around the neighborhood. I was so tired that the hill leading back to our house seemed more daunting than the Matterhorn. And it wasn't a big hill. I couldn't believe I had to walk back up that incline. With no way around it, we trudged upwards. I grabbed Buddy's arm for support. He looked at me and, out of nowhere, said, "I'm sorry."

"What are you sorry about?"

"I'm sorry you live with a husband who has dementia."

My heart cracked. "*I'm* sorry," I said.

"About what?"

"I'm sorry you live with a wife who has cancer."

I couldn't believe what we were saying to each other. We both laughed. What a pair we were! One whose brain wasn't working and the other whose body wasn't working. I cried, but I was laughing.

"Would you rather have cancer or dementia?" I asked.

"Dementia."

"Why would you choose dementia?"

"Because cancer scares me... Well, so does dementia... Dementia scares me, too."

"So, we both got the scary ones, didn't we, Bud?"

"Hmm. I guess we did."

Birthdays

At chemo #8, Dr. Mandel cautioned me that most patients with cancer as aggressive as mine would need a break after eight or nine treatments. Prior to finishing chemo #9 on New Year's Eve, he told me my healthy blood cells continued to trend upwards, creeping their way out of "low normal" into "normal" levels.

"We need to get a second opinion on you being diagnosed normal," my brother John joked when he called to wish me a "Happy New Year."

As I moved past Chemo #10 and #11 and into #12, my oncology team congratulated me. I reached Chemo #12 during the Winter Olympics and I wanted to award them with gold medals for their effort.

Our neighbor's forsythias always bloomed especially early and, looking out the kitchen window, I noticed they were slowly revealing the promise of that bright yellow blossom. I thought about my last night at twelve years old. I'd sat on the couch next to my blue-and-white portable record player and asked my sister Jayne to take one last photograph of me before I turned thirteen. The next morning we recreated the same exact scenario. I was sure the two photos would show some obvious change, capturing my transition to a teenager. But I couldn't see any difference; there was no visual evidence of no longer being a child. I asked my mom, "Where's thirteen? You told me I was going to be a teenager!"

After finishing Chemo #12, I sat for new scans at Miriam Hospital, the digital technology much more advanced than that first instamatic camera. I thought about my students, imagined them being scared that their teacher was sick. Though that thought weighed heavily on my healing, I really believed after #12 I would cross a monumental finish line and triumphantly transition off chemo and rejoin my life.

YULIANA came to Fox Point in fifth grade. On the very first day of school, she and Albertina became best friends, glued at the hip. They shared a beautiful friendship. Shortly after, it was determined that Yuliana was scheduled to be released from her Providence-based foster family. A Mormon family on a farm in Minnesota signed on to adopt her. Yuliana would work and be homeschooled with eleven other siblings. "For my going away party," she asked, "can I please have a piñata? I've always wanted a piñata."

We hung it in the center of Room 4. Not wanting the party to end, she made very limp attempts at the piñata. Yuliana wasn't prepared to say goodbye to Albertina, to Providence. She tried to be so brave, but spent most of the day smiling with a quivering lip.

The piñata string remained hung from the ceiling in Room 4 for years. Every few months the custodians asked to take it down and I would say, "No, thank you. I want to remember Yuliana and her piñata." I corresponded with her for a few months after she moved. The family sent me a picture of all twelve children posing in matching red velvet outfits. None of them were smiling. Eventually I got a final letter from Minnesota: *Please don't write anymore. It's time for Yuliana to move on. This is her life now.*

In 2014, my birthday was on a Thursday. The house was full of homemade cards and beautiful paper cranes from the children, teachers, and families at Fox Point. I was wobbly, off balanced, feeling detached from my body. Dr. Mandel had called to let me know the PET scans had unfortunately revealed new cancerous tumors in my abdomen and inflammation in my lungs. "I recommend you join a new chemotherapy clinical trial," he said.

Soon after, the phone rang again.

"Mrs. Kenner?"

"Yes, who's calling?"

"It's me."

"Me, who?"

"You know, Mrs. Kenner. It's me. Yuliana." It had been twelve years, but she had kept my number. "Do you remember me? Are you still in Room 4, Mrs. Kenner?"

"No, I'm sick. I'm at home, honey. I have cancer."

"I wanted to hear your voice on your birthday. Thank you again for my piñata party. Thank you for remembering me, Mrs. Kenner. I love you."

I Am Capable

DANA was my tough broad. She was feisty, born without the bone in her right arm from her elbow to her wrist. As a baby, she had been abandoned by her mother. One year we had a basketball tournament and she was chosen second to last. But to everyone's surprise, when Dana got the ball, even with her little arm, she could dribble and steal, then shoot and score. Right before our eyes she started to dominate the game. After a sky hook that won the game as time expired, she was named MVP. The chants reverberated through the gym and shook the bleachers.

I tried to embody Dana's winning spirit while my progress on the clinical trial was monitored carefully. After Chemo #16, it seemed like the medication was successful. The results showed "no progress" in reducing the tumors, but the major organs were "unremarkable." I imagined what it would've been like to tell Dana's aunt that Dana had made "no progress" and, in fact, she was pretty much "unremarkable." Intrinsically my results didn't sound like good news, but I had learned that medical and educational jargon usually pointed in entirely different directions.

Then, another scan showed growth in both my lungs.

A friend thought it would be a good idea if I reached out via Caring Bridge and introduced myself to her friend in Maine. Two weeks earlier, her friend Liza saw the doctor for a persistent cough and, regrettably, was diagnosed with colon cancer. The cancer had also spread to her lungs. She had lived a healthy, active life; most people in her family lived to be ninety, even one hundred years old. Caring Bridge gave us the chance to immediately connect and form a deep meaningful bond. Writing back and forth, we shared our stories and experiences. "I chose to let people in," I told Liza. "My strong faith and willingness to say 'Yes!' encourage others to carry me when I need to be carried. Those threads remain and stretch to new corners. Every day *you* will find something that inspires you," I reassured her. "Be ready because many of the most powerful lessons are at the beginning. My surgeon gave me the freedom not to look back, to focus on moving forward. I know it's helped my healing."

Liza and I each went for a lung biopsy in the following weeks on a Tuesday morning. At my procedure, I daydreamed about Dana pumping her little arm in celebration. I prayed that Liza had found her inspiration as well, that she would overcome the fear of her first biopsy. I barely knew Liza, but I wanted to spare her, to help her. I imagined one day we wouldn't just talk about our procedures; we could talk about all the secret coves in Maine, all the serene beaches in Rhode Island.

After my biopsy, upstairs in our bedroom, I struggled to get calm. "I'm having a hard time breathing," I said to Buddy. I physically could not take a deep cleansing breath.

He took off his watch. "I'm going to take a shower," he said.

"I just said I'm having a hard time breathing. Isn't there something you can say?" All I felt was the pity I had been trying to keep locked away.

"I don't know," he said, staring at the floor.

I got into teacher mode. "Think. When someone says they are having a hard time breathing, what could you say?"

"Well, let me think for a minute," he said, drawing his fingers along the marble-topped bureau. "I could get some medicine."

"Good idea, but I don't have any medicine for this. But thank you, though."

"What else? What else? What else?" he said. "I could get some water."

"That would be great, thank you. I'll take some water."

He smiled when he came back in with a Dixie cup. "Okay, am I done?"

The results of my lung biopsy revealed cancer in both lungs. I immediately began a new regime of more aggressive chemotherapy. Liza got the worst possible results, then she died three days later. I cried multiple times a day and most nights before I fell asleep. Though we never met, we cared deeply for one another. I was lucky to call her my friend.

Frightened, I prayed that the new Folfiri treatments would knock out the cancer, not the patient.

I am capable.   I am ca **pable**.   I *am* capable.

iamcapable.iamcapable.iamcapable.

I am capable.

I am capable. I am capable.

I am capable.   I am capable. I am capable.

i am caPABLE.

I am capable. I am capable. *I* am capable.

I am CAPABLE. I *Am* Capable.

I am *capable*. I am capable. I am **CAPABLE**.

I   capable

am   .

I am capable.

I *AM* *capable*.

I am capable.   I am c a p a b l e .

i

am

ca   **I am capable.** I am capable.

pa

ble.

i am capable.
I am capable.
I am capable.

I **am** capable. I a m c a p a b l e.

I AM **CAPABLE**.

i am capable. I am capable. I am c a p **A B L E**.

I

Am

CAPABLE.

I Am Capable.

Ia*M*CAPABLE ●

Fairness

EDWIN was a runner and a screamer. "Mizz Kennah, I've got so many hiding spots in this school and I'm not gonna tell you where they are. You're gonna have to find me."

"My gosh," I thought. "Is it too late to take a transfer?"

One day at Tockwotton, our job was to pass around snacks to the grandfriends. Edwin was told he could pass out cookies to the ladies, but not Mrs. Goldschmidt. "That's not fair," he said to me.

"What's not fair?"

"It's not fair Mizz Goldschmidt can't have any of the cookies."

"Mrs. Goldschmidt can't have sugar, Edwin. She is diabetic."

"Oh. So, her body can't have sugar? Will she have something else?"

"Yes, Edwin."

"Okay, good." He revealed to me he had a moral compass that operated on fairness.

Days later, his behavior escalated: he began to jump on the counters, throwing books, throwing my work, trampling my personal binders and folders. Drooling and face flushed crimson red, he opened a window and said, "I'm gonna jump! I'm gonna jump! You're not gonna catch me!"

"Edwin, stop jumping on the counters with your muddy sneakers!" I yelled. "Look at my important work. This is not fair!" Because of what he revealed to me at Tockwotton, I retrieved and used that concept with him. He instantly understood the connection.

"What's not fair?"

"It's not fair you're ruining my things and not following directions."

"I'm sorry, Mizz Kennah," he said, jumping off the counter, walking toward the sink to wipe his mouth and blow his nose. "You're right, that's not fair."

The one-year "anniversary" of my diagnosis was July 16, 2014. We gathered for our annual family trip at Popponesset Beach on Cape Cod. Thirty-three people from five states and four generations, including four new babies and toddlers. The beach, for me, was a state of mind: a chance to unwind and focus on the present and the important aspects of life.

While the new generation of cousins played and laughed, Buddy got up and began to drag away his chair. "Bud, where are you going?" I asked.

He looked to the children by the overturned sailboat and said, "I'm moving closer to the laughter."

My heart leaped. It was the most beautiful sentiment I had ever heard.

I'm moving closer to the laughter.

One of my favorite family traditions was pizza delivered right to our beach, my mom's treat for more than twenty-five years. Before scarfing down our broccoli with pineapple pizzas, we united in prayer and gratitude. I glanced around our circle in the sand and made sure to look at each person. The challenges of the past year were replaced as love and support passed through each connected hand, each embrace.

"It just doesn't seem fair that I have to leave vacation early," I complained to my brother-in-law Phil the next morning before Chemo #21.

"At least your body is strong enough for this treatment, Maureen," he said gently as he sliced the ripe peaches for our cereal. "You live in a time, in a country, in a state, and in a city where treatments for advanced cancer like yours are available."

Before saying goodbye to the beach, I sat under the umbrella with Tara and George and their new precious son. Once more, I moaned and groaned about having to trade our beach paradise for chemo. "My dad was diagnosed with cancer," George said, "but he never walked in the door to the cancer center. He died the day before he was scheduled for his first treatment."

My family was right. Somewhere, in some other examination room, in some other chemo chair, someone had it way worse. I had my hair, and I was healthy enough to travel with my family for a beach vacation, to accept more treatment, and then move on.

"I'm sorry the wires are so cold," the nursing assistant said while sticking the EKG adhesives to my chest.

"Oh, that's okay," I said.

"You look so calm. Can I ask what you're thinking about?" she asked. The soft afternoon light from the examination room windows shimmered off her heart pendant and into my eyes.

"Oh, well, we just returned from vacation and on my way here I saw an old student of mine working at the service station where we dropped off my car. He was working under the hood of another car. His boss told me, flat out, 'I wish we had more workers like him.' So, I was just thinking about him. He had been the kind of student who could never sit at a desk. He was too rest-less. But, he thought that the mop was just the greatest thing, so together we worked out a reinforcement plan: if he achieved his daily and weekly goals, he could carry the custodian's carpenter's belt and help push the bucket and squeegee." I opened my eyes slowly. "I was definitely known to bend a few rules for the good of my students."

"That must be such an integral joy of teaching." She sighed.

"What do you mean?" I asked.

"Well, that hope that what you accomplished together plays an important part in their futures. And that at some point, you witness it. Don't you think? That's why it's always important for our teachers to never give up."

We locked eyes. "Gosh," I said, recognizing for the first time how young she was, "you must be a really hard worker."

"Thank you," she said, blushing. "I am. My teachers encouraged me that I had the right qualities for this job. A lot of my friends teased me because I went to a vocational high school, but I showed them. I got this job the day I graduated. I knew I wouldn't get a chance to go to college. And now, my friends think it's no fair they never get to see me. But the truth is, every day I get to go to a job that I love."

My heart was reopened. All the paths I traveled continued to intersect with models of empathy, compassion, and hard work.

Roller Coaster

Daniel presented the idea to form a team and participate in the Alzheimer's Walk at Coney Island on September twenty-first. It made me proud that he took such an interest in his dad, advocating alongside the Alzheimer's Association. When Buddy was diagnosed, Daniel said, "I know it's going to be hard, but I need to know everything. I want you to tell me." Daniel devoted months to forming our team, *Buddy And Me*, and raising money to benefit Alzheimer's and dementia efforts.

We all gathered in our purple shirts on a beautiful day by the boardwalk. Daniel organized thirty-seven people, consisting of family, Buddy's childhood friends, and Daniel's friends from college and neighbors in Brooklyn, to stand alongside Buddy, confident and comfortable, as he received special recognition at the podium.

"Jacob 'Buddy' Kenner, an entrepreneur, small business owner, and dedicated teacher of theater, is a loyal fan of the San Francisco 49ers, Notre Dame, and Bob Dylan; a devoted son, husband, father, brother, friend, uncle, and grandfather. Buddy's infectious spirit and deep love for his family have inspired and encouraged us to be a positive influence on our community."

During the walk, I overheard Bud complimenting me to Daniel's friend Ollie. "My wife's been taking care of me for the last, you know, however many months, and uh, you know, she's a remarkable woman. I tell her how lucky I am to have her by my side. If I ever need someone by my side, it's her. I don't have to worry about who's got my back. She comes to every one of my, uh, meetings with every doctor."

Then Daniel came up behind me and suggested we ride the Cyclone. "Maybe we should just face our fears and let it all out!" Neither of us were fans of roller coasters but I seriously considered the possibility we could release all our concerns just by riding the Cyclone. Could it really be that simple?

"Don't put me on anything operated by a man with no teeth and no engineering degree," Bud said.

But Daniel went through with it. "It was awful," he said, "so I kept shouting Beyoncé's name to give me strength."

ALEJANDRO was a hard nut to crack. The "difficult" students had a special place in my heart because I knew I learned from them and they from me. He was one of my high-flyers, but I just couldn't get through to him; he considered me a pain in his neck. I knew deep down he had potential but from kindergarten to fifth grade he missed the equivalent of two-and-a-half years of school, absent sixty days alone in fourth grade.

One day, a student came to me in the hallway and said, "Ooo, Mrs. Kenner, somebody wrote something bad about you in the boys bathroom." There, in perfect, clear handwriting on the wall I read, *mrs kenner is an ass whole and the hole world thinks so.*

"Oh my gosh! That's Alejandro's handwriting!" I knew it well; he had a very floppy hand and a poor grasp but I couldn't believe how neat it looked! Our occupational therapist and I had worked for months practicing techniques and strategies to help him gain the strength to write. At first, I was embarrassed. Then I thought, "Wow, this handwriting is great. This is progress! I need my camera, this is a writing sample!" I never knew when he was going to be absent so I got as many writing samples as I could.

In the hallway, I said, "Alejandro, may I see you for a moment?"
"Huh …?"
"May I see you for a moment?"
"Wha …? Wha'd I do …?"
"Well, the good news is your handwriting has really improved. I'm proud of your handwriting — the handwriting on the wall. The bad news is you messed up your homonyms. It's 'Mrs. Kenner is an asshole. H. O. L. E. And the whole world thinks so. W. H. O. L. E.'"

~

"Scans continue to show no reduction in the size or quantity of the tumors in your lungs," Dr. Mandel said as I finished Chemo #30. I felt the damage of those eighteen months and didn't feel positive about the path forward. It was harrowing. There were so many different things that needed to be covered and I just didn't have the foresight. And with the neuropathy in my feet, I just couldn't find my footing. I thought back to the night of O.J. Simpson's Bronco chase when I had explained to my principal that I was doubting myself because many teachers I respected had recently transferred out of Special Ed.

"We're not done fighting," Dr. Mandel said, snapping me out of my reverie. "We can lower your doses to draw back the awful side effects. We'll help you regain your physical and emotional momentum. Or we can shift gears. There is a new Phase 1 clinical trial that focuses on your genetic KRAS mutation. We can try to get you in line *but* because your genetic makeup is unique…" As I mulled over the decision to trade my current neuropathy and nausea for the trial's risks of the possibility of vision loss and heart problems, I didn't hear most of what followed. "Mutations…Complex… Rare…Modifications…There are other alternative medications to consider. New discoveries are happening all the time. There's a universe of options and standard chemotherapy treatments are only a part of that universe."

Uncomfortable and disoriented, I blurted out, "It feels like I'm riding the oncology roller coaster!"

I had arrived at a critical juncture in my cancer timeline. As I drove home, I thought again of the fears I had shared with my principal. She took that moment to let me know she admired me. "I would be honored for you to be my grandson's teacher," she said. Her grandson was the light of her life. It had been the exact the push I needed to give me the confidence to know I was on the right path.

By Route 95 north, my eyes got lost in a billboard with huge letters, each filled with beautiful multicultural faces:

G.R.A.T.I.T.U.D.E.

Holiday Blues

TRAVIS was homeless. He and his mom lived in her car. He probably hadn't had a shower or a hair wash in a very long time. What that boy had gone through in his young life, what he had gone through before he came to Room 4, was horrifying. He was damaged because of it, physically, behaviorally, emotionally, mentally, and academically.

Before "No Child Left Behind" became a federal law, I taught with that motto. I never ever believed there were throwaway children, that children could be disregarded. I thought I could save them all. I really did. And if I couldn't do it by myself, I was determined to enlist as many people as possible in the effort. That was one of the best assets of my teaching: I was never that arrogant enough to think it was just me. I took pride in building a strong team, asking for what I needed. It was always about helping me help the students. A caring adult in a child's life—someone who was fair and respectful, someone who saw their potential, someone who could navigate the system—could legitimately give them a strong foundation for their future lives.

Travis came to me by way of the Providence Director of Special Education. She and I made many difficult decisions together and she introduced me to Ina Hughes' poem *A Prayer for Children*. One fall, I got a call from her asking for a favor. Though Room 4 was full, she needed me to take Travis; he was in crisis and needed a way out.

"If anybody can do it, Maureen, you can. I just need you to help me out until a seat becomes available at Harmony Hill," which at the time was a school for children with mental health disorders, emotional disturbances, and severe behavioral issues. "I would guess it would be about a month."

What a month it was. The classroom was foreign territory to Travis, and he took to it like a feral animal just out of the woods. After a month, she called again. "The seat hasn't opened. Can I ask you for another month?"

"Yes, of course."

We worked and we worked, and in the third month, right before Christmas, she called once more. "All right, Maureen, it's time. Harmony Hill has a seat. I'm going to withdraw him."

But, after talking with the principal and my Room 4 aide, and then with Travis and his mom, I made the decision to keep him in Room 4. My gut told me he had to stay. It was Christmas and he had never had a Secret Santa. I called her back. "He can't leave. He's just starting to trust me. Just starting to make friends. It's Christmas. Give the seat to someone else."

So, he stayed. He stayed for Christmas, stayed through the winter. It was a difficult winter. Travis had a rough coating. He was raw, not childlike in the least. One cold morning, he ran out the East Street door. I knew I couldn't run as fast or as far as him, but I followed my first instinct and tried anyway. It was the only time in my career I was called into the principal's office to be reprimanded. A teacher is not supposed to run after a student. The faster a teacher runs, the harder and farther the student will run. The police found Travis in a graveyard next to the housing projects crosstown, lying on a beaten-up gravestone.

Sitting at a desk was never productive for him, so I tried to build in behavioral rewards for the physical outlets he needed. If he could stay on task through a lesson, he was rewarded with ten minutes in the gym to shoot baskets. One day, I let Travis know his ten minutes were up. Not wanting to leave the gym, he went into a full-blown rage. He tore off through the hallway and when the principal tried to stop him, he nearly pushed her through the plate glass window. "Maureen," she said, "pack up his things. Today's his last day." At school, once a child physically lashed out at an authority figure, all respect was lost.

Years later, I heard Travis dragged a young girl into a bathroom and sexually assaulted her. I had a lot of guilt about that poor girl. I felt very connected, deeply affected, partially responsible. I always tried to see the good in the fact that I said, "No, he can't go. It's Christmas." I was proud of that decision then, but often second guessed myself for what happened later.

I learned to do my best — my very, very best — and surround myself with people willing to go the extra mile to put the child's needs first. The reality, however, was sometimes my best wasn't good enough. The reasons were as unique as the problems the children brought into the classroom. It broke my heart that I couldn't make a different path for Travis. Room 4 was a detour, a nice one. But it was a minor detour. Stickers on the chart were not enough. Secret Santa was not enough. It was not enough to give him Christmas.

~

Holidays were more lonesome after Buddy's diagnosis. I was the type who dressed colorfully for the holidays; I fancied the rituals, ceremonies, and celebrations, and my clothes marked all the holiday seasons. Loud and proud, that was me. That was Buddy, too. But now, every holiday came and went without recognition nor expression of love: Valentine's Day, my birthday, Easter, Mother's Day and Thanksgiving. "Happy Holidays" is an oxymoron when you are married to someone with dementia or living with aggressive cancer. Gone were the thoughtful paper hearts scattered around the house, the fresh flowers in every vase, the romantic getaways and dinners, the "Queen for a Day" treatments. Bud was barely aware what day of the week it was; anticipating and planning for the holiday was out of the question. Preparations of any sort were my responsibility now.

My friends from support group whose husbands were in more advanced stages of Alzheimer's or dementia said it was important to be fully engaged and grateful for the present. "Time will come when these will be the good old days," they said.

During Advent, a couple of workers unloaded fresh balsam trees after Saturday night mass. A few of the trees looked small enough for me to handle, and though fatigued and hesitant about tackling the decorations, I bought one. The two older men working the truck put down their coffees and offered to tie the tree to my car. After I tipped them, I saw them share the money with a homeless man. I finally felt the Christmas spirit and got excited about having a tree. I anticipated getting my home and heart ready for Christmas but, when I got home, Bud was too nervous to carry the tree inside. He forgot where the boxes of decorations and lights were in the basement. When it was time to put it in the stand, I held the tree upright, giving him one-step directions, feeling the tension mount.

He left the room. I heard the front door open.

"Bud, where are you going? I need you to help me put the tree in the stand!"

"I'll be back." He walked outside, without his coat, into the cold December air.

"You don't get to just walk away from this! I can't walk away from this and neither can you!" I leaned the tree against the wall, sat down in the sunny den, and began to cry an angry cry. "It's not Buddy. It's the disease. It's the disease."

I wondered what it must be like for Buddy, wanting to escape the normalcy, the routines he once mastered but which were now confusing. Did he know he was forgetting? Was he frightened or nervous? Worried he was losing himself, his abilities, his strength?

It had always been Bud's job to vacuum up the needles after we took the tree down. He would blast Bob Dylan and make patterns in the rugs. My tidy husband. Orderly, organized. Ship-shape. But this year he forgot where we kept the vacuum. Then he couldn't get it plugged in. Couldn't figure out how to vacuum the dried balsam needles and empty the vacuum bag. It was demoralizing watching him try to untangle most tasks. Dementia robbed him of those basic capacities. Its intrusion into our lives had started slowly, but had gradually taken hold before we were ready. It was gaining on us. Dementia detached him from his goals, disconnected him from his life story, and separated him from his — our — future. The holidays just made it even more clear how much we had lost.

Weather Conditions

I got out of bed and decided to put the car in the garage to avoid scraping off the ice with my cold, sensitive hands. The news was reporting several more inches of snow on the way. It seemed like so many winters ago that Buddy would go and warm up the car for me before school. It was such a small but thoughtful gesture.

Drooped over in the cold driveway, clinging to its roots, was a bright yellow daffodil. "I should bring you inside, let you warm up before the snow comes," I thought. But I realized it hadn't had the chance to fully blossom, so instead, I said a little prayer that it'd survive the storm.

≈

The snowdrifts were piled high enough to block every street. The roads were narrow and treacherous, I couldn't see what was coming around the corner. That winter felt like a metaphor. I had been on thin ice for four months: snowed under, hibernating, barely coping with the side effects. Perhaps, then, it was no surprise that my cancer had a snowball effect. It grew in size and significance.

According to my doctors, the likelihood of me going back to teaching was getting slimmer and slimmer. Dr. Mandel, Dr. Sanfred, and the rest of my team wanted me to focus on my—and Buddy's—health. "It would be wise to be home," they all agreed.

I didn't see myself as a retired person. I didn't see myself as being done. I had a lot more passion, a lot more to accomplish.

I didn't want to leave the routine, the kids, the support staff, the community partners, or, with Buddy never working again, the income. My dad always said, "You retire *to* something, not from something." I wasn't prepared to retire to cancer and dementia.

I tried changing the way I looked at it. If indeed I had to retire, I wanted the job to be available for the April job fair. I wanted a teacher to make the conscious choice to go through the rigorous application process, to want Room 4 as his or her dream job. I pictured myself meeting the new hire, helping set up the classroom. I knew dealing with the retirement board, the union, the school department, and the pension process would take me three to four complicated months and I didn't want to miss anything. I wanted to do it right. I wanted the satisfaction of passing the torch.

REESE had developed escape mechanisms and would lie down wherever he was: the hallway, the cafeteria, the boy's bathroom. I told him, "There's only two places in the school you can lie down; on the nurse's cot and, if I allow it, on the back rug with the pillows and stuffed animals." I believed in shaping behaviors; it was the students' job to help me understand what they needed to get back in the game. But one day, when recess was over, Reese refused to get off the top of the jungle gym. I didn't like to highlight his disobedient habits while his peers watched, but unable to move him myself, the gym teachers climbed up to get him. It escalated into a game of cat and mouse. Reese scrambled right and then left and all the while they tried to box him in. It was a fiasco. I was running out of steam.

"Reese, I'm leaving!" I yelled, taking my keys out of my purse.

His face lit up. "Missus Kennuh, can I have your keys?"

"What?"

"Can I use your keys?"

"Yes. If you come down right now, you can help me unlock the door."

Back to being old buddies again, he gave the gym teachers high fives. "Hand 'em ovah, Missus Kennuh," he said, tumbling down the fire pole. He marched the students all the way back to Room 4. He was so strong he almost broke the metal lock while figuring out which was the right key. When the door opened, he lassoed the key ring around his fingers and whistled like a gunslinger after a standoff.

Whether it was power or trust, my keys ended up being what could get Reese out of any sticky situation. If he started to have a meltdown, I'd pull them out and say, "In case the library is locked, can you help me?" Or, "I need to pick up a box in the supply room, can you help me unlock the door?"

One day, while finishing lesson plans, a substitute principal walked into Room 4. "I'm sorry to bother you, but there's a student of yours who won't get off the gym floor and the teachers are about to bring in the next class. I need you to come down and help."

"Do me a favor?" I said. "Tell him you're filling in for the principal and you need help opening the door to Room 4. Here, take these keys." He just stared at me, perplexed. "If it doesn't work, I'll come right down. Just please, lock the door on your way out."

Sure enough, when he handed Reese the keys, Reese commanded the students to quickly make their way up the hallway. Unlocking the door, he burst into Room 4 with green mucus dripping down his nose, went to his desk, sat down, and picked up a pencil.

The principal's mouth hung open. "Do you realize you've unlocked a secret," he told me at lunch. "You have the keys to success. Better yet, you found the keys to Heaven."

I noticed the daffodil again getting in the car to drive to Miriam Hospital. Blanketed in heavy snow, it stood tall, dangling its bright yellow baby bud high over the white ground.

I knew my health was declining, and perhaps going alone for the very first time was my way of sparing my support system even for a short while. It had been two years since Buddy's diagnosis. I was mindful of the constant support we had received and recognized the concern and efforts of people I didn't even know.

When I arrived at Miriam I gave Drew, the valet, my keys. I thought, "How odd and sadly comforting that I know the names of so many people here." That day, I met the new addition to my team: my palliative care doctor, Dr. Gabrielle Eirny.

"Usually after CT scan results like you've received, my patients begin to ask about prognosis," Dr. Eirny said. "Are you ready to have the difficult conversations now?" I liked the way she worded it, giving me a heads up something hard was coming. I started fidgeting in my seat. My legs became wobbly. Dr. Eirny explained the cancer, once again, had grown. I grabbed the armrest of my chair and shuddered.

"What are you saying?"

"At this rate, I would guess you might have about a year."

The room started spinning. This was the conversation I never wanted to have, never asked about, never imagined. I knew I believed in Heaven, but I wasn't sure what it was. I knew it was synonymous with something special, earned, deserved. It was a positive idea and I was sure I might qualify. "But, please, not yet," I thought.

One year? I tried to imagine what those words meant. One year.

"Are you saying I might have only four seasons left?"

"It looks like that might be the case. But with aggressive cancer like this, we can never be certain."

All I could think about were the four seasons, each one coming and going, possibly the last. Spring was right around the corner. So was my birthday. Only one more of each season? Only one more birthday? I couldn't picture what that meant. "Are you talking about four seasons? And then … and then … that's it?"

She shook her head sympathetically. "Yes, we think so."

Then it hit me. My heart started pounding.

"What about Daniel?" Was she saying only four more seasons with Daniel? We had too much to share. I never wanted to miss anything in his life. What would happen if I hadn't finished parenting him? My mind rushed with memories, vying for my attention and a piece of the moment's meaning.

I thought of a former student, Stella. She just didn't want to leave at the end of the school year. The lights were off, the desks were up, everything was off the wall and the bell had rung. "Stella, we have to go. I'm leaving. I'm going to celebrate with the teachers. It's time." And yet, another year, everything was reversed; after all the kids had left, I frantically ran up the hallway. "Wait! Wait! Come back! I forgot to teach you how to tell time to quarter past the hour! I forgot to teach you how to make change for a fifty-cent piece!"

Now in Dr. Eirny's office, I felt like Stella and that former me, all rolled into one: being forced to leave but knowing, with my limited time, that I'd chase after Daniel to share all the knowledge he'd need. "I forgot to tell you about what to do when your child turns one! I forgot to tell you about parent-teacher conferences. I forgot to tell you about how proud of you I was when you ..."

I always knew I wanted to be a mom. Always, always. I thought I would have many kids, and with Room 4, I certainly did. But I wanted children of my own as well. When Buddy and I started dating, he already had Jesse and Aaron. It became a blessing to have young stepchildren in my life as a stepmother figure, but I knew I wanted more. I knew it was going to be Daniel all along. Well, in all honesty, I also thought it was Lucy for a while, but the closer we got to August, I knew it was Daniel.

"Is Daniel ready to lose his parents?" Dr. Eirny asked.

"Of course not. No," I said. "I want him to have what I had: two parents there for all the momentous occasions." I started to cry. "Daniel made me earn every mother-of-the-year badge I wore. I love my life, and Daniel's enriched that life. He could possibly lose both of his parents in a short time. It's so sad. It's so sad. When two people are as connected as Buddy and me, it wouldn't surprise me."

Dr. Eirny reached out and held my hand. "We can make you comfortable. We are here to help you and your family. You are not alone."

"What about Buddy?" I paused. "In a way, it's good he doesn't know all that is happening. On the other hand, I can't fully share this with him. And what about my mom? What about my dad? What about my brothers and sisters? What about Jesse and Aaron and the grandkids? What about Room 4?"

What about the word "next?"

I had two doctors' appointments over the next two weeks. After each, the doctors asked to schedule follow-ups. Like everything was normal.

"What's a good day for you in August?" my dental hygienist asked.

"Let's put you in for some time next year," said my dermatologist.

It was dreamlike to have these conversations. Life would go on. I didn't bring up the fact I might not be able to make the next appointment.

I thought about all the days I signed out in our school's main office. "Have a nice afternoon. See you tomorrow," I'd say to Mrs. Stone.

"Unless God has other plans for me," she'd respond.

"See you in August," I told the hygienist. "See you next February," I told the dermatologist. "Unless God has other plans for me."

DANIEL, you were everything I hoped for, and you helped me understand children are a gift from God. "Holy cow," I said to Dad. "We got married in hurricane Gloria and had a baby during an earthquake. What the heck?" We looked at the babies in the nursery wrapped in their blankets, and their pink and blue hats. I knocked on the window to get the nurse's attention.

"Need help finding your son?" she asked.

"I don't need help finding the cutest baby in the room," I beamed. "We've already bonded for twenty hours. I breast fed him to Whitney Houston's 'Greatest Love of All.'" I pointed to the bassinet and the nurse wheeled it over.

"My gosh, he is handsome," she reaffirmed.

"Thank you! Thank you!" I was Sally Field on Oscar night, over the moon. I looked down to check the stats but didn't have my glasses on. "What does that say?" I asked.

She leaned closer. "Baby Boy Demarco."

I had picked the wrong baby! The wrong bassinet! Funny enough, the Demarco family owned a fuel company and delivered to our neighbors. If the Demarco Oil truck drove by while you and I were butting heads, I'd mutter under my breath, "Daniel, your mother and father are here!"

When you were a newborn, I watched you in awe and amazement. I often stopped to take notes. I wanted to capture and remember all your firsts. I was on maternity leave for two years. It was such a blessing to be home with you. We had so much fun but I experienced many uncertainties. The world is a chaotic place when you're a parent to a new child. Being a mother was a high-octane job. The little things, like giving you a bath, scared the daylights out of me.

You gave a lot, even as a baby. You appreciated, you giggled; you were active and persistent. When you smiled, you looked like an old man with no dentures. It was the cutest thing. I wanted to see that smile again and again. When you were only weeks old, I took you for a walk on a great fall day. We walked down Cole Avenue where it was flat and I could push the stroller with ease. I looked at you and thought, "Holy cow. What are we going to talk about?" You looked right back at me. You had really good eye contact from early on. I wanted you to hear my voice, so, as we walked, I told you all about your new neighborhood, your new world. "One thing you're going to notice about these trees is that the leaves will change. We have something called seasons. This is fall. There are four seasons."

As a young boy, you played all the time. You didn't need much—blocks, Legos, art supplies, a football or a Wiffle Ball bat—and outside I'd find you in the bushes catching grasshoppers and frogs or on the street running and diving. Like Dad, you idolized Joe Montana and Jerry Rice. You were into Ninja Turtles, Batman, Ghostbusters, and practical jokes, booby-trapping the house like your other idol, Kevin McCallister. You took pride in your process. You didn't need things instantaneously. Everything you did had a creative element; you infused our home with characters, funny impressions, and performances. In your head, you were a prankster, laughing and joking. In your heart, you were serious, strategic, and inquisitive. You thought nothing of it to ask the lifeguard to wear her hat, her whistle, to sit high up in her chair. You'd ask the pilot for a few more minutes in the cockpit. You wondered why the announcer at the Pawtucket Red Sox game wouldn't let you into the booth to call the game "Just for an inning!" When Dad ran the theater department at RISD, you always wanted to be on set talking to the actors, handling the tools, trying on the costumes, watching from the wings and every angle of the auditorium. You had a father who was proud of you and thought you were special. He saw things in you before you realized them yourself.

We taught you how to work as part of a team. As a teenager, you wore your uniforms proudly, whether it was Little League, Mock Trial, or All Children's Theater. You had many wacky coaches and they called on you in the intense moments. "Kenner! Pitcher's mound!" Back straight, shoulders out, you never batted an eyelash. No matter how embarrassed you might be to admit it, you always looked over to me on the bleachers with a look that screamed, "Mom, stop talking to the parents and pay attention!" On the brink of an undefeated season, you struck out three in the bottom of the ninth with the bases loaded. You could get a job done with very little warm-up. Other times, you practiced relentlessly. Mock Trial always gave me heart palpitations. I was so proud of how articulate you were, going downtown to the Superior Court House with slicked back hair, a blazer a size too big, and Dad's briefcase. You had prepared for both the prosecution and defense. On stage at All Children's Theater, I watched you learn who you were supposed to be as you took on great roles like Lysander and Jean Valjean. Your strengths were well suited for a life on the stage. You believed in rich texts and had an ability to look beyond the surface. It seemed you needed to play to tell a story.

As a young adult, I worried about the detours in your life. Acting was a career with many letdowns. You knew that and you chose it anyway. You believed in your creativity, your voice, your exploration of the things you couldn't see but questioned. I watched you cry after your breakup with Sarah, the woman you thought you were supposed to marry. It was the day I got a second opinion from Memorial Sloan Kettering. Your breakup was not supposed to be your story and Sloan freaking Kettering was not supposed to be mine. You attended many of your best friends' weddings as a single young man; heard their parents give toasts, watched them dance with their mothers and fathers. I wanted to be at your engagement, your wedding. I watched you play with your nieces and nephews, help them jump off the diving board, and I could just see the flash-forward of you raising your own children. It broke my heart. I wanted to see another grandchild. But through it all, we helped each other heal by continuing to participate, to clap, to laugh, to get silly, to be smart, to commit, to give back to those less fortunate.

Sure, I would have liked to trade you with Baby Boy Demarco on more than one occasion, but you were supposed to be my son and I was given the task of being your mom. My adrenaline kicked in a lot as your mom, there was a lot of feeling like it was Christmas Eve. I had a lot of hope being your mom. On the other hand, there were times I looked at you and wondered, "What kneejerk reaction is going to come out of your mouth?" Just like your father. There were times I waited for the other shoe to drop or the phone call to come that you got yourself in a deep pickle. There were many, many times of deep hurt. You need to know. You don't need to wallow in it. You need to know you can be someone who feels things deeply but you don't have to trample over somebody's heart.

Through traditions, through rituals, through children, through art and music, you will figure out a way to keep Dad and me present for all the celebrations. You'll stop and think, "What would Dad do ... What would Mom say ... Dad would really like this ... Mom would be mad if I did this ..." Rent a beach house with your cousins and buy extra lobster rolls and mojitos for us. During Christmas sing-a-longs assign me "seven swans a swimming." Totally laugh. And totally cry, too.

I wanted you to like that I cared. I didn't ever want you to think you didn't need a mother. My job was not done. I wanted you to know what I learned. Character matters. Family and kindness matter. Art and respect matter. Faith matters. It is not about the end product, but the effort. I passed you the message that you were capable, loved beyond measure, and that you had the great responsibility to keep our family strong. You are our legacy, Daniel.

SPRING

The Month Of June

JUAN was in a foster home until Rene, a single dad, adopted him. Juan was as sweet as a teddy bear but he had learned a few troublesome habits, stealing included, at the foster home; we worked hard to help him refine some of those behaviors.

In 2003, I received a registered letter from the superintendent notifying me that Rene had nominated me for Providence Teacher of the Year! The rigorous application gave me opportunities to reflect on what I believed. As Teacher of the Year, my message to others was to search constantly for new ways to be inspired and to always remember the inspiration behind choosing the profession. Was it because their parents taught them the value of education? Was it an enthusiasm for knowledge conveyed to them by one of their teachers? Or another teacher who took the time to share a good book during lunch? Or one who helped get them through the awkwardness of middle school? Maybe a teacher had instilled in them confidence that they didn't know they had? The chance to work alongside colleagues who would help guide them? A calling to service?

I was one of four winners for the City of Providence.

I was honored to represent Room 4, the teachers, and the families with whom I worked. Daniel was graduating high school and I thought, "I'm doing this for Daniel so he will always be confident in following his dreams."

In the written portion of the nomination, Rene expressed how grateful he was that he and Juan got to interact with Buddy and

Daniel at Pasta Night and other school functions. "I learned how to be a better father by watching the way you were with your own family," he wrote.

That was the highest compliment I ever received and I carried that pride with me when I submitted my retirement papers a day after Chemo #44. I asked Buddy to come with me, just as I had been with him when he submitted his name to the school board. "I want you to hold my hand. I want you to tell me I did a great job. Help me. Let's cross this finish line together."

"I'll wait here in the car," he said.

"But I want you to walk in with me. I had chemotherapy and all the side effects are acting up. Look at me, my face is purple. Please, I'm handing in my retirement papers. I'm scared. I'm proud. I'm conflicted. Please come in."

"It's okay. I can wait here."

So, I went in alone.

The woman in Human Resources seemed genuinely excited for me. "Congratulations," she said. "Thirty-five years! Boy, oh boy. What are you going to do now? What's on your list?"

"My health is at the top of my list. And my husband's health."

She spotted my chemotherapy port. "Oh, I'm so sorry." She came over and gave me a long hug. She must have also spotted the enamel cross pin on my purse because then she took me by the shoulders and said, "Most people think of Jesus as strong until the end. I think of Jesus being exhausted. He was dehydrated. When you're at the foot of the cross, it's hard to see the resurrection. You need to believe in your capacity to keep going. You may feel alone but you're not. God will be there in ways you can't predict."

I went out to the car and Buddy smiled and asked where we were going to lunch.

～

"Are you going to want a retirement party?" my friends at Fox Point asked later.

"Of course, I want a party! I want a parade down Wickenden Street!"

I didn't want to go out quietly. I had dear friends who brought disposable cameras to school on the last day, took some pictures, and left. I wanted to celebrate! But even though they offered the party I always wanted, I couldn't visualize myself attending.

～

The month of June was about school send-offs and goodbyes.

At the beginning of the month, I went to a school board meeting and signed up for the right to be heard.

"Good evening. My name is Maureen Kenner and I am a Special Education Teacher at Vartan Gregorian School at Fox Point. It is with bittersweet emotions that I have submitted my name for retirement from Providence Schools. My husband, Jacob Kenner, a retired Providence teacher; our son, Daniel, a Providence Schools alumnus; and my niece, Laura, are here with me tonight. Together, our Kenner family has more than sixty years of proud commitment to the Providence School district. More than thirty-five years ago, I graduated from Rhode Island College on a Saturday in May. Two days later, I received a call from the Providence School Department asking me to sub for the remainder of the school year. I had plans to travel with my sister after graduation and told them I was unavailable. I'll never forget what she said: 'Can we count on you for the fall?' Thank you for helping that young college graduate fulfill her dream as a Special Education teacher for the past thirty-five years. Please continue to put best effort and practices into everything you do. Remember the faces of the appreciative staff, families, and children to help guide your important decisions. We are counting on you! Thank you."

"I've never heard a thank you from a teacher before," a school board member said, stopping us as we left.

"I needed you to know I am honored that we have been able to count on each other all these years," I said.

At a stop sign, driving away from the school department downtown, there was a frantic beeping from over my left shoulder.

"Mrs. Kenner! Mrs. Kenner! Is that you?" the driver called out the window.

I looked over, and there was Dana, my tough broad, her little arm curled around the wheel. She waved to me and sped off, fluttering and laughing.

On a cold rainy night, I was invited to the last PTO meeting of the year. When the time came for committee sign ups, I caught myself raising my hand to volunteer. Several times, I had to pull it down. The last item on the agenda was "Cake and Photographs." Former PTO presidents whose children were in middle and high school came to the meeting to say thank you to me. A parent, whose son had cancer, left the hospital to see me off.

Later that week, at a magical celebration for teachers in the botanical gardens at the zoo, I was given special recognition. Seeing my name in the retiree portion of the program was absolutely surreal.

That weekend, I dug out my favorite drama club shirt and attended Fox Point School's sixtieth birthday bash. We barbecued and ate cake, danced and celebrated with many of the veteran teachers who came back for the festivities. I sat on the bench under the shade in the playground and talked with families and connected newer teachers to my legacy programs—the Rainbow Connection at Tockwotton, Brown Science, School Improvement, PTO, and Teachers on the Estuary.

Hours before the retirement party, I went with Buddy and Daniel to Tockwotton. As soon as I walked into the room and saw the grandfriends, the kids, and the staff, I cried. I was so emotional to leave one of my favorite programs. I only knew two of the children from Room 4. They weren't Mrs. Kenner's kids any longer. I was sliding farther and farther out of the picture. I was there, but separate.

That night, I dressed up for the party and chose my outfit around a Mother's Day necklace Buddy had bought for me years ago. Every time I wore that aquamarine and peridot drop stone sterling silver necklace, I thought about the important moments that lit up my life, especially since the stones were mine and Daniel's birthstones. My stomach was in knots. I was weak. But when I stepped into the banquet hall, it was like coming home. Everything softened. My best friend pinned a corsage on me. I looked her in the eyes and let myself smile. I was, at long last, comfortable in my own skin again.

Fox Point planned a magical, love-filled evening. All the teachers who played a major part in my life when I was younger mingled with the people who knew me for the last twenty-seven years. I was proud to have them all as mentors and friends. I gravitated toward other teachers that went the distance and were in it for the right reasons. I wanted to emulate them, to find my passion and my joy the way they had.

Patricia, a librarian at Fox Point Library, and I talked about Lawrence, who we'd both had as a student. I recounted the day I walked into the library and saw a beautiful drawing crumpled in the trash, which I recognized because our art teacher had been working on Post-Impressionism. I took it out of the trash and tried to smooth out the wrinkles. It was extraordinary—a sailor in an expansive, tumultuous sea at sunset. Lawrence had been sitting alone in the library. That was his place of respite, and he was the last child there every night after school. I asked him about the drawing.

"My mother doesn't want me to bring home my junk anymore," he told me.

Patricia left her desk and walked me back to her office. The walls were full of Lawrence's discarded artwork. He later went on to receive a scholarship from Brown University and had the chance to work with Robert Ballard, the oceanographer who retrieved the *Titanic*.

At the retirement party, many teachers and parents made speeches, taking the microphone to share such genuine anecdotes.

"I told Mrs. Kenner, 'Lighten up, it's Christmas! And she said, 'We have to hold on because the kids go wild at Christmas!'" my teacher's aide said, laughing. "When you went into Room 4, you were expected to wait, unless it was an emergency, because her focus was hyper-vigilant on the students. She had very high expectations. Coasting and mediocrity were not accepted. From herself, or from the students."

"This is a school and a staff that cares about the kids and about each other," my sisters whispered before I got up to speak. I reached deep into my heart to let everyone know how grateful I was for the tribute. I was so proud to feel that my work, and my spirit, had made a difference.

"I knew at a young age what I wanted to do," I said, "and I was able to live my dream. The deeper I got, the more it reinforced my belief I was where I was supposed to be. To all the hard-working and fiercely passionate staff, we have always been able to count on each other to do the right thing for our children. Thank you. We learned from those who came before us and will leave a legacy of professionalism long after we are gone. Thank you for continuing to give your best effort both in and around the classroom each and every day. To the younger teachers and staff, by taking the torch, you've given us retirees peace of mind. Thank you for jumping on board to contribute your time, talents and treasures in helping make our community a better place. We are counting on you to stay the course. You too can finish the race with dignity and grace. I am counting on you to work hard, stay inspired, be kind, and do your very best for each other and our children."

Clapout

VARMA and his family escaped the war in Liberia. He was my student mayor. As a result of an attack on his mother, he came into the world under horrible circumstances; he was born with muscular dystrophy and an autoimmune deficiency. He used a wheelchair for long distances but was able to get around the school with a walker. Wise beyond his years, he loved textbooks and assignments, but he also had a stubborn, defiant streak.

One day, Varma was in the "think about your life choices chair" when it was time for recess. But he refused to move. He took his sweet old time while we were all lined up, waiting for him to get his act together. By the time we got outside, the other classrooms were already in the field, the teams already chosen for kickball. Varma wasn't the type of kid who sat in the dugout; he always wanted in on the action. He inched over to the field in his walker. "They've already started the game, they're not going to let him play," I thought. "Maybe I'll go over and ask the outfielders to let him have a turn." But then I thought, "This isn't about you, Maureen. Everything they need to learn about school happens at recess."

When I looked over again, Varma was at home plate. They had let him come up to bat. I went to the fence and watched the play unfold. He kicked the ball and walked his walker to first base. The second baseman missed the ball so Varma rounded first to second. When the outfielder overthrew the cutoff man, Varma scurried from second to third. The cheering got louder. I realized what was going to happen. Kids celebrated along the third baseline as Varma, gasping, rounded the base toward home. Home plate flooded with a parade of his peers clapping and reaching out for high fives as he crossed it; he took his hands off his walker and pumped his fists.

I started to cry. I walked over to my colleague, who was also crying, so proud of her class for including Varma. We put our arms around each other. "This is why I do this job," she said. "I am so blessed to be here to see this." It was fulfilling to be part of a school where *that* was success, *that* was greatness. It wasn't measured by accountability or state tests, but by the children's purest actions.

At Clapout, Fox Point's version of a graduation celebration, all the classrooms line the hallways while the fifth graders march through the school to rock star applause. The little guys wave to their recess buddies, bus friends, and reading group partners as they take their first steps as middle schoolers. The procession ends in the auditorium with speeches and songs. The principal asked if I'd be the guest speaker. It was a very special honor.

I went to Room 4 to say goodbye to the kids, to my beloved aides, and to thank the substitute for his care of the children. One last surprise was in store: I was going to walk in the Clapout.

When the music started, I got in line behind the kids. "Who's that?" one girl squeaked.

"She's the one we're supposed to give the flowers to!" They knew me only as the lady in the pink dress.

I marched through the school to thunderous applause. There were many faces I did not recognize, but they were all so precious in their navy uniforms, sweaty from cheering. I made eye contact with everyone I loved and worked with and made sure to high five every hand. I got so many hugs and went through many tissues. By the time I got through the hallway, I was Miss America with her huge bouquet of long-stem flowers.

The auditorium was full of parents and grandparents. I didn't have any notes but I felt right at home holding the microphone again, just like I had done for drama club. I looked at all the faces and realized it was my chance, my only chance, to say goodbye to the kids. I had gone to the school board and the PTO meeting. I had seen the grandfriends at Tockwotton and been thrown a beautiful party by my colleagues. But this moment was my chance to focus on the kids.

"When I was your age, I knew I would be a teacher when I grew up. I could think of no better accomplishment than teaching a child to read or helping them see themselves as inventors and thinkers of big ideas. I am honored to have been a teacher at your school. I was confident that my students always knew they could count on me to do my very best. And I am counting on you to do smart work and to help make the world a little bit brighter each day."

I made sure the important voices of my past resonated in what I said. I listened for Principal Everett, Principal Brooks. I heard Dr. Vartan Gregorian. I heard Robin Hearn at drama club. I spoke on the themes the students had helped me learn over the years that proved necessary during my illness. It came out right, and right from my heart.

"Expect a lot from yourself and allow yourself to dream. Choose hope and accept help from others. There are values you must remember to help you continue to grow in middle school. The first is perseverance. I'm positive that from your time here, you learned how to spell it and you learned what it looks like. It's up to you to be an eternal optimist and a cheerleader for your friends. Always remember compassion and tolerance. Be respectful of individual differences and remain curious about the unique personalities of all your peers. Don't be fearful to interact and work with people who look different and who act differently than you. Choose to do the right things for the right reasons. Often, while on the sidelines, I stood proudly, watching with delight acts of compassion and friendship our students displayed toward each other and toward members of our community. And for that, I will always be so proud and remain optimistic about the future."

At the reception, I looked around the cafeteria and noticed it wasn't my moment any longer. The families were focused on their kids and the kids were focused on their friends. It was time to go. This was the moment, the last goodbye. With an armful of flowers, I took a deep breath and then Buddy and I walked out the door.

"What's next?" I said. "I'm not ready to go home."

We sat outside Duck and Bunny café on Wickenden Street, drank iced tea, and had lunch. Buddy wasn't able to give me feedback, or share his pride, even though he had coached alongside me for most of my career. The silence was deafening, like white noise ringing after a concert. My world separated.

Buddy told me once that in retirement he wanted to open a lemonade stand in the Bahamas. He pictured me in a pretty little sundress in a thatched roof schoolhouse with children running around. It was symbolic of going somewhere warm and light and breezy, doing the things we loved. As we got older, and more realistic, the goal was to retire when we paid off the mortgage. There would be financial freedom of some sort, to travel to countries we had yet to visit with one another, pursue volunteer work, and spend time with the grand-darlings as they grew up.

Our dreams of retirement were never clouded with health is-sues, for either of us. The life we worked toward was not there; it had changed past the point of recognizing. The reality of what I was retiring to was obvious. "Will I be ready in his time of need?" I thought. I worried about that all the time. What would happen to Buddy when something happened to me? What was going to happen to me when something happened to him?

I lost my role as a teacher, my legacy left at the door. It became just another Friday afternoon. I sat on the café patio thinking about how far I had come. It had been a beautiful month, jam-packed with capstone sendoffs; each event had brought such a deep sense of satisfaction. It was my last day of school, unlike anything I had experienced before. Fox Point welcomed five new staff members, including a new teacher for Room 4.

Time To Move On

Once the school year ended, a colleague offered to help me box up my classroom, my home-away-from-home for twenty-seven years. Practical and decisive, she provided reassurance during a very emotional time. She labeled several large storage containers, according to their destination: "KEEP IN ROOM 4," "DONATE TO MAGGIE'S NEW CLASSROOM," "DANIEL," "TOSS." Room 4 was an organized hodgepodge of mismatched furniture, teaching equipment, and outdated technology, but beautifully busy, with lots of color and exemplary student work.

In college, I volunteered in a pale mint-green classroom with nothing on the walls, just a flag and an intercom system. The teacher believed that children's minds were too distracted. He wanted their attention only on the work. I thought that was a little extreme, so I did the opposite. If their eyes and minds were going to wander, I wanted every corner of the classroom to spark thought and wonder to feed their brains and imaginations.

My colleague and I made our way through the bookshelves to inventory the math, science, and reading materials that needed to stay in Room 4. I hoped the abundance of excellent math manipulatives, science materials, and the diverse classroom library would prove valuable to the new teacher. I missed the books. Books were important members of Room 4: those read-aloud books, the books in a series, my book buckets, constant, loyal, and always ready for an adventure. Our niece Laura had a friend, Maggie, who was opening her very first third-grade classroom, so I left suggestions on how to use my reference books most effectively. I thought about her opening my well-loved copy of *Guiding Readers and Writers*, by Irene Fountas and Gay Su Pinnell. I hoped that my notes, written on colorful, torn post-its scattered through the book, would benefit her students. And I hoped she would remember being proposed to in Room 4 by one of my students on Valentine's Day 2006 when she visited as a thirteen year old. (There were pink frosted cupcakes, chips, and heart-shaped chocolates for the reception.)

We sorted through my personal items and made decisions about where to send them. I boxed up many of the books and games Daniel had lent me from his collection over the years: *Treasure Island*, *The Merry Adventures of Robin Hood*, *King Arthur and the Knights of the Round Table*, *The Giving Tree*, and *The Polar Express*.

Dana, my tough broad, came to mind again. She always connected with deep moving texts. She cried harder and harder as we moved through Patricia Polacco's *Pink and Say*, about two teenage Union soldiers from different backgrounds trying to survive in Confederate territory during the Civil War. But Dana was still trying to be my tough broad. "I just have something in my eye. I'm okay." At the end of the book she raised her hand. "This is the saddest book you've ever read to us. I can't wait to ask my aunt to get it for me for Christmas!"

Going through Room 4 was like taking a slow stroll through the years. Stuffed animals, beach chairs, coffee mugs, magnets, puppets, mismatched puzzles and board games, the prize bag and wrapping paper for when a child wanted to gift the prize to their mother, calculators with loose buttons, lab coats stained from pig heart dissections, Brown University Athletic T-shirts, bags of extra clothes for students in need, holiday decorations, flags, ancient artifacts, heart-shaped rocks, twelve colorful plastic leis, the birthday crown, sour gum and Jolly Ranchers, glitter, fancy scissors, packs and packs of motivational stickers (mostly empty), "No Homework" coupons, deflated kickballs, Wiffle balls and bent plastic bats, jump ropes, sidewalk chalk, *National Geographic* magazines, fancy computer paper for publishing parties, burned-out electric sharpeners, near empty bottles of hand sanitizer, and an endless supply of markers, all of which were dried up and useless, except the scented Mr. Sketch, the Energizer Bunny of markers. I gave one pack to Maggie, left one pack for the new teacher, and took a pack home for myself.

We moved to another book shelf, peeled back the map of the United States shower curtain—floor to ceiling filled with binders, each representing an important chapter in my professional and personal growth. Lee Canter Assertive Discipline, lesson plans, School Improvement Team minutes and agendas, community partnerships with Brown Science, Save the Bay, "I Was There" Fox Point Oral History, Teachers on the Estuary, Tockwotton Home, drama club scripts, Eye to Eye legacy, PTO, Teacher Evaluations, RI Alternate Assessment, Special Education regulations, Character Education, Site-Based Management, Balanced Literacy, Core Knowledge, Multiple Intelligences, Math Matters. I went through them all, deciding it was best to leave the new teacher an empty bookshelf. It was a hard decision.

Finally, I stood in front of the closet where the photographs hung, the Wall of Fame. Many were peeling now, browned with curly, ripped edges, smudged from pressing on their smiles and holding onto their childhood. I looked at each photograph, remembered each face and each story and began to doubt whether I could finish. I wasn't ready to say goodbye.

My colleague stood with an empty trash barrel. "Maureen, it's time," she said authoritatively. "Keep those memories in your heart, but it's time to move on. Take the photos off the closet."

"How can I throw this away? Remember the time this sunflower hung in the art show…They got the gold at Special Olympics that year…This was the last photo taken before he went to Butler Hospital…This was taken right before his mother died…"

"If you do this for every photo, we'll be here until Labor Day."

Less than twenty-four hours later, the phone rang. It was an Arkansas area code. "Mrs. Kenner?"

"Oh, Yuliana." She had the same sweet voice.

"Do you remember when you brought me to the grandfriends? I got my Certified Nursing Assistant certificate and am working in a nursing home. I love it. And guess what? I'm a mother! I have a baby boy! But how are you feeling, Mrs. Kenner?"

"I had to retire from Room 4 because of my health. I'm so glad that you called because I was just thinking about you. There was a picture of you and Albertina on the Wall of Fame. It was taken on the first day of fifth grade. You both looked so beautiful. Suntanned, in crisp, white blouses, each with your hair tied in matching bows."

"We still stay in touch," she said excitedly.

We reminisced once more about her piñata party. "I left the string hanging in Room 4," I reassured her.

"Thank you, Mrs. Kenner. I think of you all the time. Thank you for being my teacher."

Uncertainty Meet Courage

Dr. Eirny looked at me and said, "I think we are approaching the end of your life."

There were complications that could come on very suddenly, without warning. There was a chance that after Chemo #55, I was sicker from the chemo than I was from the cancer. My neuropathy could lead to a lack of mobility; "the functioning statue," Dr. Eirny called it. I wrestled with the idea that I was knowingly putting something in my body that could take away my independence. I took the chemotherapy to prolong my life. But what kind of life would it be? It was the first time in two-and-a-half years I was really afraid. Dr. Eirny cautioned I should focus on living, not, as she said, "on the details of toxicity."

At home, Daniel asked, "Do you feel like a woman at the end of your life?"

"I feel physically sick. My body is changing," I said. "There are discomforts and complications. I don't have stamina. I can't juggle mental tasks. I'm afraid I won't be strong enough to make the right decisions. Afraid I'll continue to lose more control over my life. Afraid what is out there to help might come too late. Afraid of not being ready. I am not at peace and I don't know where to put my feelings or from where to retrieve that level of support. It's really scary for me. Is a season a beginning or is it an end? I don't know. It's a bell that can't be unrung."

I looked at Daniel. I thought of the weekend we drove to Attitash Mountain when he was only six. Memories, clouded by the hallucinogenic nature of the chemo, blurred like a French Impressionist painting. I remembered watching Daniel on a chairlift, looking at his smile caught in the folds of the autumn landscape.

Daniel put the big blue couch pillow in his lap and patted it, urging me to lie down. "I hope you realize how much of a role model you've become to everyone who knows you," he said, throwing the brown fleece blanket over my feet.

"I can honestly say the way I'm going to live the end of my life is pretty much how I've lived my whole life." I closed my eyes. "I've always believed in things bigger than me. I'm fascinated by the holes in shells, rocks that look like hearts, how the ocean works…I'm captivated by them."

"Well, then, since we really only have a limited time together, let's be sure to find more moments in the light together. How does that sound, Dad?"

"Yeah, just listening," Buddy said comfortably from his corner of the couch by the CD player. "The light comes in when the blinds are crooked."

"That's absolutely true, Bud," I said, craning my neck toward him. "What else are you thinking?"

"Oh, what you were saying is pretty accurate." He was so content, so agreeable, fighting through everything that was expected of FTD; that was not what the disease was supposed to look like.

"What did you agree with, Dad?"

"Well, she said she thought it was going to be something, but now that it's something else, that something's not going to happen anymore," he said, closing his book. "But, if you're up for it, you and I go can still go for our walk."

"Sure, Dad. Some sun will feel good." Daniel kissed my head

and stood up. "We'll be back," he whispered to me. I was really proud that each of us, in our own unique way, contributed to Buddy feeling loved. "How was your TV show last night, Dad?"

"Oh, it was very good," Bud answered, zipping up his blue fleece.

"It was a good season finale?"

Bud smiled, arching his eyebrows. "It didn't seem to be going in the right direction. She was getting on a plane to leave him and he was in a little café for a cup of coffee when she walked in. He told her he loved her and when she heard those words, she knew he was the guy, so they had a nice long kiss and that was the end."

Daniel's palm was spread on his father's shoulder as they made their way to the front door. I pictured Daniel one day teaching somebody to throw a football the same way Buddy had taught him as an adolescent. "I could go for a happily ever after," Daniel said.

"Absolutely," Bud replied.

"But I don't think our family is going to get that."

"No. No, I don't think so," I heard Buddy say just before the door closed behind them.

Although reluctant to begin one more round of Folfox after my conversation with Dr. Eirny, Dr. Mandel strongly recommended it was the best option to increase the quantity and quality of my life. I thought about our niece, Laura, one of the strongest people I knew. For months she had trained for, and had completed, the Chicago Marathon. She had joined other teammates to raise money for cancer research. A man in the crowd had waved a sign that read "UNCERTAINTY MEET COURAGE" while Buddy and I cheered from the finish line.

"You are my inspiration," our glowing marathoner said, hugging me, after victoriously stretching her arms as high as they'd reach.

"You are one of mine, Laura."

I was not going to give up. I was still in the game. Even if I was on the bench, I still wanted to be in the game.

"Sign me up," I told Dr. Mandel. "I'll be there."

A Good Sunset For A Cowboy

Daniel came home the week after Father's Day to celebrate with Buddy and spend time with Laura, who had just completed her MBA from Providence College. Buddy, Daniel, and I spent Monday, June 20, 2016, at the Seekonk Swimming and Tennis Club. We had lunch upstairs on the deck and Daniel read his Father's Day card to Bud. After lunch, we swam, lay in the sun and let ourselves feel that sense of freedom that comes at the beginning of summer. I loved scheduling trips to concerts, fireworks, and beaches, so I had sent Daniel lists of "The 10 Best Places in Rhode Island to Watch the Sunset" and "The Best Places in Rhode Island for Ice Cream."

"When I visit, Mom, let's try the sunset list. Let's start at number one."

So, on Tuesday, June 21, we walked the water's edge at Colt State Park with Bud and Laura. We walked along the paved road, gazing over the sparkling panorama of Narragansett Bay. The neuropathy had permanently settled into my legs and feet and it felt like trudging a muddy trail in heavy Army boots. I had a biopsy scheduled for the next day on one of the tumors in my abdomen. We had waited months and months for new immunotherapy trials. The biopsy was to see if I qualified for a new study from Japan. I was apprehensive and felt lousy. The tumors in my lungs pressed up against the walls of my ribs and I felt the wheezing, hacking cough coming on.

"Go ahead without me," I said to them. "I'm going to stay here and rest."

I hated to slow down, but I knew I couldn't keep up. I found a bench, on which the inscription read *To Marian, For Being a Good Wife and Mother*, and watched the three of them walk along the rocks until they were out of sight. I lifted my face to the sun and prayed for strength for the days ahead. For me. For Buddy. For Daniel and Laura. That we would each find our way, alone and together.

As they continued to walk down the gravel path, past the playing fields and picnic tables, toward the scenic overlook, Daniel asked Bud, "You think Mom's beautiful?"

"Oh yeah."

"A good teacher?"

"Oh yeah."

"Good wife?"

"Oh yeah."

"Good mom?"

"Oh yeah," he said, his smile broadening.

"What's your favorite thing about Ro?" Laura asked.

Buddy looked out across the water, squinted, and then relaxed his shoulders. "She's got the most beautiful smile of any woman I've ever met. When you're with her and she's with you, you know that the two of you are together in a very, very special, sweet world." With the sun right on his face, Buddy said to himself, "This is one of the best days of my life."

We all indulged in clam cakes, seafood casseroles, and watermelon mojitos for dinner. We toasted to times shared and to times ahead. Afterwards, we dashed off to Sachuest Point National Wildlife Refuge for a glorious pink sunset over the Atlantic Ocean.

Laura and I made daisy chains for our hair. Daniel had child-like energy and giddiness as he skipped toward the observation platform.

"You know what, Dad? I know what you mean," Daniel said. "This *has* been an incredible day."

After the biopsy the next day, the doctors recommended rest and no heavy lifting. Daniel and Bud went to the Pawtucket Red Sox game, another summertime favorite, and sat in the second row behind home plate. Buddy called balls and strikes. Looking into the crimson red sunset, Buddy told Daniel, "That is a good sunset for a cowboy."

Daniel headed back to Brooklyn on Thursday morning, and Buddy went to Fruit Hill Day Care Center for the day. Run by the nuns, my Jewish husband was very at home there. He loved the structure. I stayed home to rest and spoke with my sister Jayne about the week. "I feel like I've lost all control of my life," I said, in spite of all the excitement we had experienced. I struggled to reconcile with the sadness and the melancholy I felt.

When Bud got home, he presented me with a picture he painted: a sea glass green vase of red tulips. He then went for a walk, as he always did. I watched him from the kitchen window. I was happy he could still enjoy his walks down Fosdyke Street and Elmgrove Avenue. He looked so handsome in his new Father's Day cobalt blue golf shirt, bright against the neighbors' budding trees.

When he returned we headed to Fox Point Library to get the stack of summer reading that our librarian friend had put on hold for us. We picked up pizza, and an order of chicken wings for Buddy, on the way home. I waited in the car while Buddy got the food. At first, he went into the Japanese restaurant next door. A minute after he finally made it into Hope Street Pizza, the owner came out and tapped on the car window. Apparently, Bud had been confused about the order. I appreciated the way our neighborhood small businesses gave Bud extra help when he needed it.

We ate in the den and binged the last few episodes of *Suits*. "I'll get the ice cream," I said when we finished. "Will you get the laundry from the basement and we'll meet back in the den?"

I was standing at the open freezer when I heard it.

SLAM! SLAM! SLAM! SLAM! BANG!

"I fell!" Bud cried out. "I fell!"

One of his new Birkenstocks sandals was halfway up the basement steps. He was lying on his back on the hard cement floor, arms out by his side, palms up. The clean laundry covered his face.

"I fell. I fell."

I got to him in seconds. "I'm here, Bud. I'm here."

Daniel's blue bath towel laid beneath his head, soaking up the blood. "He needs stitches," I thought.

"Bud, look at me. How many fingers do I have up?"

"Five. You have five fingers, Ro."

I watched the tan in his face turn to gray, like a window shade pulled down from his forehead. There was something unsettling about the way his palms lay wilted and floppy. I reached for them. "Bud, can you feel my hands? Squeeze my hand, Bud."

He couldn't.

I called 911 from the landline in the basement, then ran from room to room, grabbing whatever I could think of: two fleeces, two water bottles, and the Power of Attorney papers. I barely noticed the pain, the exhaustion from that morning's biopsy.

"We'll get him some stitches for the gash and be home later," I reassured myself.

Trauma rescue arrived within minutes. I rode with Bud in the ambulance in case he wasn't able to give the information they needed. The NBA draft was playing on the radio and, for a brief second, I tuned in. "Have the Providence College basketball stars been drafted yet? Kris Dunn? Ben Bentil?" I asked the EMT stabilizing Bud on the stretcher.

"Was he able to move his hands after the fall, Mrs. Kenner?" he replied, snapping me back to the scene.

"No. He didn't move his hands after the fall."

Our ambulance arrived at the Rhode Island Hospital Emergency Room at 7:30 p.m. They triaged Bud in the hallway in front of the opening and closing electric doors. Right there with the drug overdoses, the heart attacks, the drunks, the gun injuries, the vomiting, and the bleeding.

"This is the busiest night of the summer," a paramedic hollered to the front desk as he ran past.

I stood by Buddy's side, weak and frightened. Hospital staff scurried around us. I got the distinct impression that everyone thought someone else was attending to us. Panic was brewing.

I texted Daniel. *Are you still working? Can I call to say goodnight?*

I called my mom. It went to voicemail.

I was alone, scared and unsure of what to do.

"He's not moving his hands!" I shouted. "He's not moving his hands!" At change of shift, three hours after we got there, I caught the attention of a trauma nurse, who looked me in the eyes, unsettled.

"For how long has he not moved his hands?"

"Since he fell!"

She hurried out and quickly returned with two neurologists who examined Bud and rushed him to a critical care room. In order to stabilize his neck in a collar, the nurse cut off the cobalt blue golf shirt. She tossed it to the ground, his handsome Father's Day gift, thrown out with the rest of the night's medical waste.

I started to cry, to shake, feeling the overwhelming urgency of what was happening. This was more than stitches. Clutching my stomach, I thought I was going to vomit.

I left a voicemail for my sister Jayne, who called back later when she got out of the theater. She called Dianne and, before Dianne even hung up, my brother-in-law Phil packed electrolyte water, granola bars, and his Green Bay Packers fleece blanket and headed out the door. "Tell Maureen I'll be there by 1:30 in the morning."

Buddy always saw Phil as another brother. On the morning of Jesse's wedding in 2007, Bud got flustered trying to finish his tie and Phil came in to help. "You might be the most handsome man at this wedding. After Jesse, of course." A beautiful light came through the blinds while Buddy talked to Phil about how proud he was that his firstborn was getting married.

Phil and I spent an intense night in the Critical Care Emergency Room with Bud. Everything happened in slow motion. We met staff, listened, questioned, and deliberated; I spoke with nurses whom I could tell had an obvious passion and calling for emergency medicine. Rhode Island Hospital was nationally recognized for superior critical care services. It was also the only hospital in the state dedicated to the treatment of neurological patients. At 3:00 in the morning, I heard loud machines outside the windows. "It's an odd time to be mowing the lawn," I muttered.

"That's no lawn mower," a nurse said matter-of-factly. "That's a helicopter bringing in another trauma victim."

A neurologist spoke to us about Incomplete Spinal Cord injury; Buddy had decompression of Cervical discs 1-8 and

Thoracic 1. These controlled the functions of breathing, heart rate, head and neck movement, shoulder movement, wrist and elbow movement, and hand and finger movement. Each disc was like a shock absorber for the spine, enabling the neck to handle various stresses of movement. Bud was moved to the Neurology Critical Care Unit (NCCU) in preparation for a spinal fusion; a metal rod would be attached to the front of his spine and screwed to each vertebral bone as a way to promote the healing process. The director of spinal disorders for the Department of Neurosurgery and the surgical director for the Comprehensive Spine Center would lead the team.

I pictured Buddy walking down our street in the cobalt blue golf shirt. "Was it just yesterday?" I thought.

At Bud's bedside in the NCCU I had to sign consent forms. I tried to listen carefully to the doctors but was overcome with frenzy and exhaustion. I hadn't slept in over thirty hours. "I'm sorry," I said to the neurosurgeon. "I can't follow what you're saying. Can you please explain to my brother-in-law what you want us to do?"

The doctors were hopeful the surgery would return his functioning to the levels before the injury, but I was also cautioned that results post-surgery varied enormously from person to person.

I held Bud's hand. He looked at me. It seemed like he was trying so hard to stay focused on what was happening.

"What should we do, hon?" I said, dreading the surgery.

"It sounds complicated," he said, "but necessary."

Bud was wheeled off to surgery within the hour.

~

We were instructed to go home, sleep, and meet back after the six-hour surgery. My mom had routinely treated us to a housecleaning team and they showed up to clean the bloody steps and basement floor before we got home.

Worn out and weary, I sat in our yard with Phil and Daniel, who took the first train that morning out of Penn Station.

"This is exactly the kind of day Bud would sit out in his chair," Phil said.

"Relaxing quietly and reading his book," Daniel continued.

"Watching his birds," I finished.

Daniel and Phil made the phone calls so I could sleep. Our beautiful, cozy home felt strange and disturbed in a way I had never experienced. I showered for what seemed like hours, washing myself over and over with the Philosophy shower gel that always brought me comfort. With all the strength I had left, I leaned on the wall. I cried — deep, anguished cries.

I settled into bed with clean pajamas and my bathrobe tied tight. The summer sunlight poured through the windows onto our bed. No matter how hard I tried, I was unable to relax. I kept hearing Buddy falling, slamming, shouting, "I fell! I fell!" I could not shake the horrors of waiting and waiting and waiting in the emergency room alone before Phil arrived. I reached over to Bud's side of the bed. "Will you ever sleep in bed with me again?" I wondered. I thought about getting up to sleep on the couch; it was just too sad lying there thinking about him, alone.

YOSELINE was hardened by eleven years old, but there was so much sadness under her rock-hard surface. She never had a mother and never had a bed in the same place for more than a few months at a time. She came to Room 4 via the state educational advocate. "We have a foster care child and we need to find her a school placement immediately. She would be a good fit in your classroom."

Later that year, the end of Reading Week culminated with Pajama Day. A guest reader was in the center of the gym where there was a full-blown pajama party. The teachers and faculty sat in their favorite chairs, I was in my rocking chair, and the children, in Ninja Turtle and ruffled princess pajamas, were spread out to every corner of the gym. Cozy and safe. Yoseline wore a scuffed yellow onesie with little ducks. She held her stuffed hippopotamus and a pillow. Like all of us, she took Pajama Day very seriously.

The gym phone rang. It was Mrs. Fuller asking me to bring Yoseline to the office. There was a court hearing that day that would decide whether Yoseline would be reunited with her mother, so I hoped there might be good news. I walked her in to a tiny conference room full of adults looking at their feet and shuffling stacks of paper. Yoseline was asked to sit outside the door.

Yoseline's mother had cleared out her home and never showed up to the courthouse. A neighbor reported that she'd left early that morning in a U-Haul. Yoseline was not going home. They were taking her, in her yellow duck onesie, to her fifteenth foster home. I received this news, one of the most painful moments of my career, standing in the doorway wearing a bathrobe. "Go to Room 4, get her backpack, and meet us in the office to sign the consent forms."

"You want me to tell a child who's wearing duck pajamas that her mother broke her promises and disappeared without saying goodbye?!" It was outrageous. I unloaded my anger on my colleagues, as if they were responsible. I spun on my heels and marched to Room 4. I loaded her backpack so full of markers, crayons, stationary, glitter, glue, stickers, candy, and gum that I couldn't even zip it.

Back in the office, I told the administrators, "She needs to say goodbye to her friends."

"No. We have to leave now." I wanted to scream in protest, but outrage turned to heartbreak when I knelt down to give Yoseline her backpack. I guided her head in to the nook of my shoulder so I could hold her. She cried so heavily I felt her tears seep through my bathrobe. "This is not the news we hoped for," I whispered into her ear.

"Mrs. Kenner," she sniffled. "It feels like there's a monster in my closet."

"Oh, honey," I said, combing my fingers through her hair. "I need you to continue to be brave. You haven't been allowed to follow a typical path. But I've always admired that about you. And that's why I feel like we were put together. And time and time again, you've proven that you have all of the traits a mother would want from a daughter. This is not your fault. I will always be here to take pride in all your accomplishments. I love you, sweetie."

Dragging her hippopotamus stuffed animal, Yoseline walked to the front door and I walked toward the gym. We did that thing people do when they don't want to be the first to stop looking back. It was excruciating. I always wanted to be the teacher who thought like a mother and there was another mother who chose to abandon her child. I cried so hard I began to choke.

The gym was full of pajama-clad children listening to the reading, hugging their blankies. I sat in my rocker, frozen. For a brief moment, I allowed myself to imagine what it must have been like for Yoseline's mother to have made that choice. Devastated, I tried to empathize with the woman who had made such a despicable decision, but I couldn't. Yoseline was not going home to her mom. I was forever changed.

Will You Ever

The doctors spent the first few hours after surgery at Bud's bedside. We were shown scans of Bud's spine and guided through expectations. He had sensation, though minimal to no movement, in his shoulders, arms, hands, fingers, legs, and toes. The good news, at least, was that Bud was able to breathe and swallow on his own. A team of neurologists took turns assessing him every four hours and nurses came by every two.

"How do you feel?" Jesse asked his dad.

"I feel sad."

"What's making you sad?"

"I'm sad we're not at home."

Family and a few close friends showed up to join us in the NCCU. Aaron came from Charlottesville and Bud told him, "I hope I can get strong enough so I can wrestle my oldest grandson and he won't beat me." The Handwergers came with enough lunch from their Ocean State Sandwich Company to feed the entire hospital. Although they were no strangers to heartache and physical challenges, I knew it was difficult for them to see Bud hooked up to machines. However, we found moments to laugh and have a good time. When the Handwergers left, Bud turned to Daniel and said, "He is a great friend. He is my brother's brother. The kind of guy who would rather beg for forgiveness than ask for permission. I've always gravitated toward people like that. That's how I lived my life. No relenting. No repenting."

Jesse, Aaron, and Daniel headed to lunch. Buddy told the doctor, "Okay, we're going to have to finish up now. I need to catch up to those three. Let me take my boys to lunch." That sounded like the perfect idea for my husband: to walk off his injury alongside his three sons.

Laura was finishing her last MBA obligation so I decided not to tell her about Uncle Buddy's accident. I just didn't want to intrude. Eventually, Jayne called to tell her as she wandered among her memories on campus. Laura came straight to the hospital and spent the next day by her Unc Bud's side. She, Daniel, and Buddy played word association games. We started to hear simple yet profound expressions from Bud.

"Hot or cold, Uncle Buddy?"

"Hot."

"Longboat Key or Cape Cod?"

"Cape Cod."

"Heaven or Hell?" Daniel asked morosely.

"Heaven."

"What do you think Heaven is?" Daniel said.

"It's where my mom and my dad live."

It was time for Laura to say goodbye. After living near us for six years, she was moving to Cape Cod to begin her job search. Laura and Daniel stood by Buddy's bedside; they understood the concept of avoiding "the long goodbye" for someone with dementia.

"Unc Bud, I'm going to do some errands now," Laura said. "I am so proud of you. Remember how you supported me at the Chicago Marathon? This is going to be your marathon. You're going to have to work really hard. You're going to have to do your exercises to get your strength back."

"I can do that. And if I'm in the gym working, do you think that'll be somewhere I'll be happy?"

I sat in the lounge chair by the window, shivering under the Green Bay Packers fleece blanket, watching Buddy lovingly gaze up at Laura. "You are a star," he told her. "You have always been a star. Daniel, you always want to have a star by your side. A star like her."

~

The doctor moved his thumb and pointer finger into a C. "We need our thumbs a lot," he said to Buddy. "We have to get you to move your thumbs, Jake. I know it sounds simple but you have a big job ahead of you."

One of our dedicated nurses told Daniel and me how important it was for us to get fresh air and some rest. To move around and stay hydrated.

"While all eyes are on Jake, you need to take care of yourselves."

We found the lone small patch of still sunny grass just outside the hospital. "Let's lie here in the sun for a few minutes before we have to go back in there," Daniel said. I rolled up my skirt to let the sunshine warm my freezing skin and stretched out next to him. I visualized that moment between Daniel and his grandmother Roz in the courtyard years earlier and wondered, "How'd we get up this high? How'd we get this far, pushing, emerging, evolving through life?"

"I want to go back to the pool club and sit on the deck and have an ice cream sundae together, as a family," I said. "Does it make me selfish to want more? I've gotten my head around the idea that that would be enough for me. I don't have the big bucket list we never accomplished. I don't need the fancy trips. Of course I wish we could go to Greece and Italy and Spain. Of course I want to go back to Ogunquit. I wish we could make love in the middle of the afternoon, but I always felt like my life was enough for me. There is going to be significant loss, exponential loss, permanent loss."

We let ourselves cry.

"I'm going to have to learn how to laugh again," Daniel said after a long pause. "And this is supposed to be a good week! Next week you're back on chemo."

"Listen to us," I said, laughing nervously. "I'm just so afraid that my faith is going to be tested by this." I couldn't let Buddy down. I couldn't let my family down. I couldn't let myself down. "When we got the dementia diagnosis, we processed that," I said, expressing more of the terrifying emotions building up. "Then we got the cancer diagnosis and again we tried to make friggin' lemonade out of lemons. A falling injury has been my biggest fear. And now it's coming true. Only, I am more scared than I thought possible. More scared than being wheeled in for a biopsy, more scared than driving to my next chemotherapy, more scared than hearing the horrific stories at dementia support group. Fear and terror are in my system. I don't know if I am strong enough."

Over the years, I had seen many colleagues fall victim to burnout. At orientation one year, a colleague sat next to me and talked about anticipating retirement. "I am so close. I can feel it. I am coasting."

"Congratulations," I said. "So, this will be your last orientation!"

"No, no. I'll retire in six years," he replied.

"Six years?" I said. "You're going to coast for six years?"

"Oh, I'm so close I can taste it. Six more years is all I have to put up with."

"Do you realize six years is the entire length of the children's time here?" I asked.

I thought, "My gosh. Please don't let that be me. Ever, ever." I was very mindful how and why people, especially teachers, burn out. Teachers can only do so much, and the system asks them to do more and more with less and less. Luckily it didn't force me to quit; it forced me to think about problem solving. I was never afraid to speak up, even if it meant asking for more. More time, more money, more help. I never wanted my students to see me quit. I wanted to live by the mottos I taught: "A winner never quits...If you quit you can never win...If at first you don't succeed, try and try again..." When Principal Angeline Brooks was young, her father told her, "Yes, it's very important how you finish. But focus on running the race, not finishing."

As the sun finally set behind the hospital, Daniel suggested we begin to fill up the *Imagine* notebook with medical information and recollections from the hospital. It had been my Christmas gift from Laura. I lay there and thought about all the reasons why Bud needed to move his thumbs. It was such a simple action and goal, but it grew to immense proportions in my mind, the thought of it gaining momentum like a runaway train, until I couldn't stop thinking about what he had to do.

❧

Will you ever use a new razor and, with great precision, give yourself a smooth shave?

Will you ever flip open your glasses case and slam it shut?

Will you ever open the newspaper, hold the pen, check off your television shows, use the remote?

Will you ever zip your blue fleece, pat the breast pocket for your wallet, zip the side pocket to secure your keys?

Will you ever tie your sneakers, check the door lock, and head out for your walk?

Will you ever open a new library book and turn the page?

Will you ever carry the beach bag for me, get the noodle, and swim laps across the pool?

Will you ever move the lawn chair into the shade, fill up our water bottles, shell a peanut?

Will you ever open the tuna for me, twisting and turning the can opener when my numb fingers can't, use the spoon to scoop the fruit, bring the yogurt to your mouth?

Will you ever have a catch, throw a baseball, toss a football?

Will you ever high five, fist bump, pat Daniel's back like you did at the waterfall in Montana or during the sunset in Longboat Key?

Will you ever put on a Bob Dylan CD?

Will you ever hold the playbill at Providence Performing Arts Center, eat chocolate chip cookies during the show?

Will you ever reach for the clam cake, dunk it in the chowder, rush in for seconds and thirds before anyone notices?

Will you ever hand over twenty dollars for pizza, eat chicken wings?

Will you ever scoop pistachio ice cream, pour fudge on top of it?

Will you ever load and empty the dishwasher for me, noisily stack and chip our plates, carry out the recycling?

Will you ever rub my feet stretched out on your lap?

Will you ever walk downstairs, carry up the laundry basket?

Will you ever hold my hand?

Will we ever go hand in hand again?

SUMMER

Here And Now

For eleven days we wearily pressed on at the NCCU. We were assigned critical care teams, case managers, social workers, and palliative care specialists. We became students of spinal cord injury, MRIs, CT scans, and medication side effects. We tried to process every ounce of information from each neuro assessment, no matter how complex, and every fine grain of each nurse's review. I learned what angle the bed needed to be so that Bud could swallow his food and take sips of water. At Bud's bedside, we watched as he went through endless speech, occupational, and physical therapies. We waited, we needed, to see the improvement from surgery.

Bud worked so hard, always smiling, always agreeable. Over those first few days he was able to recover his memory about the fall and describe it exactly as it happened.

"I fell six feet of hard stairs. There were bricks and concrete. Tougher than any stage. I fell, I told Ro. This is not good. This is not good. Usually, I don't say those things. She called the night man and they took me in an ambulance."

Small moments, loaded with pure love, started to flow out of Buddy in powerful volts and sparks of interaction. It was as if he was plugged back in.

"What do you see, Bud, when you look into Daniel's eyes?"

"Happiness."

"Oh yeah?" Daniel asked.

"Yes. But you'd look better with that hat off so I can see your halo. Then you'll be ready for Broadway."

"What do you see, Dad, when you look at Mom?"

"An aura that feels like love. She is…she is…she *is* my love. Oh, those eyes so bright and blue are like daylight to me. I love you, Ro."

"Thank you, Bud. I love hearing you say that."

He had been quiet for so long, but in the hospital, he spoke more with us—spoke about his father, being a father himself, and about his grandmother. "My mom called and told me Grandma was dying. I was on a trip in Morocco. What was I supposed to do? They needed me there. I'd be anywhere for my family. That's the way I am."

Every day, Buddy gave our family the stories we hadn't heard in so long, putting a vocabulary to use that we'd all been sure he'd lost forever.

"You know, my uncle gave me his Mercedes and four keys to take to two banks in New York City," Buddy told Daniel. "There were different safety deposit boxes and inside them there was seventy-five thousand dollars in hundred-dollar bills. That's what was in there. And that was just one trip."

"Your uncle ever get you in trouble?" Daniel asked.

"A couple close calls. He never put me in a position to be involved. I was his errand boy. He thought I was loyal. And I was. He was a hundred percent right. I didn't steal from him. A lot of people stole from him. The first few trips were tests. They were. He sent me to a jewelry store to pick up a couple boxes of diamonds. I delivered every stone. That's when he came and put his arm around me. He said I was like a son."

"Tell me again about Little Abie Laveen," Daniel asked, trying to coax out the rest of a story he knew by heart.

"Oh, Little Abie Laveen? He was a merchant who walked around with a coat full of diamonds. And my uncle would store them in his safe. He had a huge safe. They'd sit and play cards for a while, then they'd go knock off joints together. They'd walk in a department store in the middle of the day, unroll a rug, and roll up Little Abie Laveen into the rug. And when the store closed and everyone went home, Little Abie Laveen would unroll himself onto the floor and let my uncle in through the front door. Jack whatever they wanted and sell it out back."

It broke my heart every time Daniel laughed with his dad. I knew the pain it would cause later. But a lot of the time it was bittersweet.

Daniel helped stir up memories of Sydney, Buddy's mentor and father figure, whom Bud followed from Tulane University to George Washington University when Sydney was hired in their theater department. Together, Bud and Sydney had worked on Jean Genet's *The Balcony* and the US premier of Arrabal's *The Architect and The Emperor of Assyria*. They'd memorized their lines as they ran miles around the Georgetown track.

"And then we went into rehearsal," Bud said. "And I'd say, 'Sydney, do you know *this* scene?' And he'd laugh at me and he'd say, 'Of course I do. What are you talking about?' The play is about these two people who are searching for themselves in each other, and the emperor is the father figure for the architect. That's what I thought, at least. And I asked Sydney, 'Are you my father figure?' And he said, 'Yeah. Not just in this play, but in your life. I know your father died when you were twenty and you have no father. I'm your father now.' So, I said, 'That's cool. Hey, Dad? Can I borrow a hundred bucks?'"

"Would you like to write a letter to someone?" Daniel asked him.

"Sure. Let's write to Jack, my father-in-law." Daniel took out a pen and wrote every word Bud said in the *Imagine* notebook:

*Jack's a great father and he has amazing children and I love
him and I love Ro. I've always loved Ro, my wife, she's my
life, his daughter, who I call my heart, and you have a heart,
too, we all need hearts. So that's the take away. She's my heart
and we love you, and I want to thank you for all of those
prayers and wishes that I love.*

Aaron and the grandkids were celebrating at a family wedding
that weekend so Bud decided to write to them as well:

*Aaron, we're going to write you a little letter. It's from Dad
and your brother and we heard you were involved with a
party and that you're having a great time and that your day
is one you'll remember for your life and that you'll have some
photographs. Please tell them to have a great day and just
know how happy we are your children are there and happy
with you and love you very much. We will get together with
you in the warm weather and we'll meet you at our house and
you can stay with us for as long as you want, you're my guest,
you'll be my guest, and you'll be Ro's guest, and we'll have a
good time together and then we'll sit down, all of us, and have
an amazingly good dinner.*

Daniel played music from his iPhone after feeding his dad
that night. Each song held such a new, profound meaning. Van
Morrison's "The Mystery" and "In the Garden." Hendrix's cover
of "All Along the Watchtower." Fleetwood Mac's "Go Your Own
Way" and "Don't Stop." And of course, Cousin Bob: "The Times
They Are A Changin'," "Blowin' In The Wind," and "Just Like Tom
Thumb's Blues." When Buddy sang along to the second verse of

"Mr. Tambourine Man," the words nearly ripped out our hearts. Daniel and I wept.

"I'll work hard to get out of here," Buddy said. "Then I can be closer to my wife."

Daniel leaned in to kiss him goodnight. Bud said, "Always keep a good song in your heart, Bucky. I love you."

"What is love?" Daniel asked.

"Love is quiet and powerful and special if it finds a home," his dad answered.

"Any advice for me going forward tonight, Dad?"

"See only what you need to see."

"So, what do you see?"

"I see a little boy in a 49ers jersey who'd raise his arms when Joe scored. A little boy who'd say 'Touchdown Joe!' You know, Bill Walsh brought Joe to the Niners from Notre Dame. And I always loved San Francisco because I'd go out west and visit my uncle and my cousins. I could find a flight there and back for sixty bucks. Kezar Stadium, where the Niners played, was right across the street from my uncle's house. My uncle Paul. Candlestick came after Kezar. So, I'd go and watch them on Sundays. I'd go to the game and I'd watch, uh, the quarterback, who was, uh, what was his name?"

"I have no clue," Daniel said.

"Brodie. John Brodie. He was a great QB, but the team was lousy. And everybody in the stadium would be smoking grass. It was in the sixties. And I would come home to my uncle, stoned outta my mind. And he'd say to me, my nickname was 'Junior,' 'Junior, Junior, I'm over here.' And I'd say, 'I'm sorry, Paulie, I just have to sit down for a few moments.' And he'd say, 'How was the game?' And I'd say, 'What game?' But, uh, I was telling a story. Oh, so, in the eighties, Joe became the quarterback. And there was a little boy, and he looked like you, and every Sunday, very religiously, he watched the 49ers on my lap. He was the cutest little companion all those years. For all those Super Bowls."

We got such profound joy and love from the man we longed for. The painkillers had turned something on inside Buddy that had been off. "I wonder if the injury knocked the dementia out of his head," Daniel whispered to me.

But we both knew that it wasn't true.

"So, yeah, of course we're going to win the Super Bowl tonight," Buddy continued, slowly closing his eyes. "Joe took us to four and won all four. And he'll be there tonight, on the sideline, because the greats, they never run out of magic."

Buddy's mind was more like a flickering light bulb, sending bursts of bright energy out to us, struggling against the inevitable dark.

Delirium started setting in—that particular daze that comes from too much time spent in a hospital. The heavy doses of pain meds began to give Bud fever dreams.

"Why did they steal the money and not investigate it?" he shouted from his sleep.

"What did they do, hon?" I asked, startled awake.

"They stole the money."

"They'll investigate and try to figure it out," I reassured him.

"Not in New Orleans, they won't!"

I got up every day, tried to remember how to put one foot in front of the other. How to eat and drink, shower and dress, how to manage the dozens of complicated decisions and next steps after Buddy's discharge. Daniel, Jayne, and I began to navigate the daunting financial consequences of such a catastrophic injury. We began by plotting a course through the Medicare process and the complicated, mind-numbing world of health insurance.

Every four hours, our family watched intently as the neuro team evaluated Bud's progress.

"Where are you?"

"Do you know where you are?"

"What day is it?"

"What year is it?"

"What's this object called?"

He lay there being poked and prodded, asked for his name a thousand times. He had sensation but still little to no movement. "Jake, scratch the sheet. Scratch the sheet like I'm doing. Jacob. Scratch the sheet. Ready, set, go."

"I am."

He wasn't.

I covered his hand with the sheet and waited—tried to pretend it hadn't happened.

Stuck in a dark place, I was filled with a sense of anger I had never experienced before. I couldn't shake the sounds of his fall. It took all my strength to just stay hydrated. I rested in the hospital family lounge, dragging the Green Bay Packers blanket like Linus to the bumpy leather La-Z-Boy recliners by the windows. I began daily prayer and meditation rituals at the hospital chapel. I prayed for strength, for healing, for the grace not to hang onto anger. I prayed I would be strong enough to support our three boys as they each found their own ways of processing and connecting with their dad when he needed them the most. I prayed I would be able to accept the things I could not change and began to prepare myself that a miracle might not happen.

Pent-up and restless, we reactivated Caring Bridge to maintain communication and received an outpouring of disbelief and support from family, friends, and neighbors, who thought of everything to help nurture our bodies and souls. My Fox Point warrior women invited Daniel to a barbecue and the Handwergers had him out to the pond for kayaking. Daniel sought counseling to desperately understand the complicated feelings of selfishness versus selflessness. His best friend, F.J., came from Brooklyn to help him search for the most appropriate acute rehabilitation facility. They toured Spaulding in Boston, HealthSouth in Braintree, and on the way home, stopped at a driving range. Bud asked Daniel to describe his best shot.

"Well, Dad, it had to be when I whacked the ball right into a rainbow."

Bud and I had seen the rainbow, too, perfectly arched over the horizon.

~

Day after day, the doctors assessed Buddy, and day after day, nothing changed. They redid MRIs to confirm that there hadn't been any complications from surgery. I detected discouragement amongst the staff by the lack of his progress, more frustrated with cognitive responses to their basic questions.

"Your husband is very impaired. He may not get to where he was. Lack of mobility and inability to care for himself will present many challenges. And when you throw Frontotemporal Lobe Dementia into the pot, well...It is best to prepare for the worst, Mrs. Kenner."

Nine days after the injury, Dr. Mandel called Daniel and me in to give us the results of my biopsy. I knew the results the minute Dr. Mandel walked in the door, shoulders slouched, eyes down, drooping. "I'm so sorry," he said, heavy hearted. "We struck out again." Nothing hopeful was on the horizon. I had indeed officially lost all control over my life.

BUDDY was released from the NCCU on the morning of July 4, 2016. Unsure what would come next after discharge to the rehabilitation hospital, my brother John, Daniel, and I gathered around Bud's bedside.

"Before we go," Buddy said, "we have to know what's important in our house. I want to talk about the here and now. Your heart is my heart. I want the pictures on the wall, all of my friends, who did not say no, to know I never said no. Tell them what's important here and now. Not what could be or what should be. My life is your heart. Your life is my heart. We're going to do this together in the here and now. And that's how I want to live our lives."

Going Off To War

PRESTON was always very special to me. I knew him outside of Room 4 because his brother wrestled on the high school team with Jesse and Aaron. Preston would cheer at the matches. When Preston was in fourth grade, his brother's car skidded on a patch of black ice; the ensuing crash killed him.

Preston's parents decided to travel to an island together to grieve after the funeral. I thought it was unusual for the parents to leave their son in a time of tragedy, but his mom later confided that if they hadn't, their marriage wouldn't have survived. Their family had a permanent place in my heart as I began to understand how tragic circumstances influence difficult decisions.

Years later, on Field Day 2004, I had just been named Providence Teacher of the Year and would be publicly announced as a winner at the Mayor's office that afternoon. I sat in a beach chair surrounded by other teachers, watching our kids run and sprint, toss water balloons, slurp Del's Lemonade, and get sunburned when a handsome man walked through the sack races.

"Mrs. Kenner!" he shouted as he came closer.

Preston gave me a big, sweaty hug.

"I came to say hello. I want to see Room 4. I want to see my desk. I want to see Mrs. Milton."

"You've never been shy telling me I'm your second favorite teacher but I'm okay with the silver," I laughed.

"I wanted to visit the school before I say goodbye."

Coming back to Fox Point was always important to Preston. He liked coming back into the room to wander, to tell me his favorite spots, to point out what looked different. I would watch him, seeing him as a ten-year-old boy.

"Where are you going?"

"I'm leaving for Iraq."

There was Preston, surrounded by all the little boys and girls playing and competing for prizes, back to see his desk, his teachers, to walk the hallways of his childhood before going off to war.

"I want to take all the memories with me," he said.

That was the first time that happened to me. I was honored he would visit Room 4 to say goodbye. But I was scared, and imagined he was scared, too.

We were pen pals for the first year of his deployment. I couldn't reconcile that my ten-year-old student, who I watched grieve his brother's death, was now a solider carrying a weapon in Iraq. When his first tour of duty was over, he came to Fox Point to let us know he was safe, that he was re-upping. At the time, Room 4 was studying the Revolutionary War.

On his next visit, he brought a beautiful woman with him—his wife. A General's daughter.

"I'm here to tell you about Proctor, our newborn son."

There I stood, a grandfriend.

❧

Buddy spent thirty-four days in rehab boot camp. We were assigned a team to set expectations and goals, provide family support, and determine the length of his stay. At his bedside, or in a wheelchair in their gym, his days were filled with therapy sessions, one after the other, speech, physical, occupational, psychiatric. He required adaptive equipment for all ADLs, activities of daily living. Buddy underwent bowel and bladder retraining and had a catheter inserted. We waited patiently through each urinary tract infection for the right combination and dose of medications to keep him comfortable but alert enough to participate fully.

Buddy was willing, but often unable, to do the therapy that would help him regain his motor functioning. We coached and cheered each attempt. Constantly fighting the pinball machine inside my body, I finally took the morphine I had been prescribed weeks before. The pain was just too much. I lay next to Buddy on his mattress while he napped, the air conditioning blasting down on us. I had filled vases with tall sunflowers to try giving the room some warmth. A physician's assistant looked at me, inconsolable, crying next to Buddy. "You're a mess," she said.

"Yes. I am a mess. How are we going to do this?" I groaned.

"You just do it," she cautioned, pouring me a glass of water into a Styrofoam cup.

"This is the hardest thing either of us has ever done. Spinal cord injury with dementia and spinal cord injury with cancer is just too mind-boggling. Too horrific to endure. It's definitely the hardest thing I've ever done. I know it's the hardest thing my husband's ever done. Spinal cord injury makes dementia look like a walk in the park."

Outside the hospital on the cement courtyard, we sat: me in the shade, Buddy in his wheelchair facing the sun. Even though I worked with the handicapped my whole life, the wheelchair always scared me. It meant less mobility, less independence, less freedom. It's hard work. For everyone. The student and the family.

"Talk to me about how you're feeling, Bud."

"I feel pretty good."

"Are you lonely here?"

"Maybe. Sometimes."

That was the first time I feared he was slipping into sadness, a sorrow deep enough to swallow his motivation to rally.

"What do you miss?"

"I miss … I miss … I miss …"

I waited three to five seconds to see if he could retrieve what he wanted to say. He was stuck, like a needle on a record. My job was to lift that needle, move it along, so we could enjoy the rest of the song together.

"The yard?"

"Yup."

"Your books?"

"Yup."

"The couch?"

"Yup."

"Me?"

"Yup."

"Our sons?"

"Yup."

"Oh look, Bud! Here comes a green convertible Mustang."

"I had one of those … but it wasn't green."

On our first date, he had picked me up in a light blue Mustang convertible. "You might want to sit closer to me," he'd said, patting the space next to him, "the passenger door is broken."

I sat next to Buddy's wheelchair on a cold metal patio chair and watched the world go by. A world of green Mustang convertibles, men who could put the top down, smile in the sunlight, flirt with their passengers, and step on the gas.

Nothing I said was helpful. I couldn't seem to reach him.

Buddy closed his eyes. "I just want to sit here in the sun right now. Nothing else."

Reports were conflicted; progress inconsistent. He often slept for hours and hours, unable to be roused for treatment, meals, or visits. Then, two weeks in, we found out he was being overmedicated, given double the dosage in the morning instead of a half dose at bedtime. We had to stay vigilant to ensure our quiet, co-operative, immobile patient got the movement, hydration, and nutrition he needed. We steered the slippery slope of involvement and micromanaging versus trusting the staff to be competent in our absence.

Too weak to drive the forty-five minutes on the highway, friends and neighbors signed up on Caring Bridge to take turns driving me to and from the hospital. They also signed up to bring me food, so that each night when I returned to Fosdyke Street, I'd find a healthy home-cooked meal left lovingly on the patio. TV kept Buddy company at night, TV filled with horrifying police shootings, wars, violence, and political strife. I insisted to the staff he only watch golf, baseball, or the nature channel.

Family and friends drove from near and far to help fill the hours and hours of tedious downtime after therapies. The grand-darlings decorated the room with colorful butterflies and designs to brighten his day. They wanted him to get up and go swimming, to run under the sprinklers, to play mini golf, to go for ice cream. Laura came from Cape Cod with a bottle of sand, shells, and jumbo lobster rolls. Katherine filled Unc Bud's memory book with reminders of their fantasy football team, *The Hazel Hellcats*, and chicken dinners during her Providence College years. One of Buddy's brothers drove from New Hampshire with fresh fruit and stories of family fun with their grandson. Buddy's best friend from

Tulane brought old photos and, upon finding bunches of Buddy's hair in the trash, educated the CNA to not comb Buddy's kinky hair. Another lifelong friend brought a video of Dylan earlier that summer performing at Tanglewood. Proud that Cousin Bob was still on his "Never Ending Tour," they watched the video over and over. My dad and Dianne were present when Buddy, harnessed on a fixed track, began to move, one foot in front of the other, with a three-person assist. "I'm part of a group here," Buddy told Dianne. "Everyone works hard as part of the group. That's just what we do."

Unfortunately, Buddy's tenacity wasn't shared by the insurance companies. "I'm sorry," the doctor said. "Forty-five days is the maximum Medicare will give for your husband's case." The news came six days before Buddy would be kicked out of the facility.

The Talk

Daniel and I began site tours of sub-acute skilled nursing facilities. I had to have Bud closer to Providence as we moved to the next stage. I needed to be able to get to him quickly and the morphine really slowed me down. I grew frail while he was at rehab; lost my independence. I was bone on bone; I could fit my whole hand around my calves. I couldn't carry a dish to the sink without feeling like I was going to drop it. Because I was not a match for immunotherapy, I required more grueling Lonsurf chemotherapy until something less toxic became available.

The day before discharge to Wingate Healthcare Rehab, Daniel and I went to Bud's last physical therapy session in the gym. He was able to take thirty-four steps on the fixed track with a two-person assist. His physical therapist seemed downhearted despite the success of the rigorous workout. "Jake is a great guy," he said with sadness in his eyes. "I wish we could have done more for him. I'm so sorry."

I watched the therapists wipe down every mat, every table, every piece of equipment. They were a motivated, hardworking team. Buddy, Daniel, and I sat still in the corner of the gym, each of us exhausted. As they began turning out the lights, it felt like last call. We were being kicked out way too soon, with so much progress to go before we could recapture all we had lost in the injury.

"Okay…okay…okay," Buddy said, coaching himself while resting to get his blood pressure back down. "So, here we go…as we go to our own environment, to work all day and all night…it doesn't hurt to be there. I think we should keep working…we should keep working…keep working, being productive." That was just his nature; Buddy was never a quitter.

After reviewing the "ready to be faxed" copy of Buddy's medical records, I got into a heated battle with one of the doctors. They were still double dosing his sleep medication and dispensing it in the morning! I thought of all those days of fatigue, listlessness, inability to comply with directions, and how that adversely affected his progress. Maybe things could have been different. Did the meds take more away from Buddy than what was already lost? I registered my complaints with the patient advocacy board and seriously considered filing medical malpractice against two staff members. I then filled out all the complimentary cards, wrote personal thank you notes to each staff person who provided real care to Buddy, and packed up his room, angry and eager to move him closer to home.

On Saturday, August 6, Jesse, Daniel, and I brought Buddy to Wingate, just one mile from home; one mile from our walking path, our park; one mile from 7 Stars Bakery and 3 Sisters Ice Cream. We helped him settle into a spacious, sunny corner room, 2418. We knew from our research that Wingate was conducive to some of our goals—it gave us a chance to bring Bud as close to home as possible, to give him a social and interactive quality of life, and a chance to bring him outside to their gorgeous gardens and patios—but we also knew moving him from an acute to a sub-acute facility had its drawbacks. We learned that although the therapists were dedicated and caring, Wingate was simply not equipped for his complex level of rehabilitation.

~

I increased my morphine to deal with the shortness of breath due to the tumors in my lungs and the pain in my abdomen. On Monday, August 8, Daniel took me to RI Hospital for another CT scan to determine if the Lonsurf chemotherapy was working. Remembering the post-traumatic memories of those horrible days with Buddy in the NCCU, both of us got Del's frozen Lemonade and toasted for a good scan. I was worried, a sadness so close to the surface I could feel it in my pores.

Dr. Mandel called us in to deliver the results on August 10, Daniel's thirtieth birthday. "Happy birthday," I said to him, walking into Miriam and up to Fain 3. "Thirty years ago, I went in to the hospital and had you, and today, thirty years later, you're walking me in to the hospital. We've had some really sweet moments in between, haven't we?" I stopped on the landing before the second floor to catch my breath. "When I was thinking about what to give you as a birthday gift, it dawned on me in the middle of the night that you gave *me* the greatest gift. You've given me a gift without even realizing it. Watching how you've been with Daddy since his fall. Watching how you are with me, our family. You've brought out the best in us."

"*And* the worst in you," he said, teasing.

"But it was all so genuine," I said. "Both Daddy and I appreciate that you are willing to fully share your emotions, good, bad, and ugly, with us. Yes, it can be devastating to watch. It breaks my heart to see, but in a very powerful, wonderful way, I at least feel blessed we can be the ones that you feel comfortable to unleash on. And I want you to always remember I *was* there with you all those years when you *did* need me. As a mom, I know I'm going to miss out on a lot, but I didn't miss these years watching you grow. After these last six weeks, I'm so confident that you have everything in place to take you another thirty."

~

One at a time, they all came in: my oncologist, my palliative care doctors, social workers, and volunteers. I sensed something in their posture as they inched their chairs closer to the examining table.

"I want you to stop taking the Lonsurf," Dr. Mandel finally said. "It's not working. The cancer is growing and causing the discomfort in your belly. It's very serious. I'm so sorry."

I felt the air leave the room. My lungs contracted and I began to cough violently, the pain pounding on my ribs. I looked over to Daniel, his eyes caught in headlights.

"Are we having 'the talk'?" I heard myself choke.

Dr. Eirny cupped my hands in hers. "Yes, Maureen. We are having 'the talk' right now. The chemo isn't working. We are all out of options. We want you to redirect your attention away from Lonsurf and focus on yourself now. Clinical trials and other options are too far down the road and it doesn't seem you will be able to meet them."

Then a sound I didn't recognize came from deep in my soul: a wail.

Dr. Mandel leaned onto my shoulder and began to cry. I always wanted to be successful for him. We had a mutual and competitive understanding that I would work hard for him and that he was working just as hard for me. "You are so brave. You have done everything right," he said.

There was not going to be a Chemo #64.

"It could be weeks to a few months. We're going to recommend you to hospice," Dr. Eirny said to me.

Daniel was stunned. His face reddened, his eyes swelled. I could not imagine what it was like for him, on his thirtieth birthday, to hear that his mom was out of options and was going on hospice while his dad lay practically paralyzed in a nursing home. What must it be like, at that age, to feel the steady decline of both parents?

"Continue to do what you have always done," Dr. Mandel urged. "Live your life. Be truthful and open. Build new memories."

~

Three days later, at the celebration for my nephew Andy and his wife's, Jillian's, marriage, the priest asked the congregation to rid ourselves from distractions and challenges, to be completely present. Watching Andy watch Jillian walk down the longest aisle in Illinois, I felt a serene sense of happiness. They chose me to do the second reading and, as I looked down from the altar, I saw such beautiful expressions of love from those gathered.

Waiting for the bride and groom outside Jillian's church, my brother John hailed down the ice cream truck as Daniel and my wonderful, dashing nieces and nephews played on the playground. We toasted with Good Humor ice cream, recalling our childhood days on King Street where we would pause every kickball game for a Toasted Almond or Strawberry Shortcake. That night, we hugged, we cried, we laughed, we posed for pictures without Buddy, and we danced and danced and danced, footloose and fancy free, all night long. We left it all on the dance floor. Out of profound sadness and terror came the understanding that Dr. Mandel was right. The only option was to live in the moment.

Dreams

In late August, I was invited for a girl's weekend at Popponesset Beach. Three generations of women — my mom, Jayne, Dianne, Katherine, Laura and I — gathered to seek summer's parting pleasures. We recharged, reconnected, collected seashells, admired the spectacular dahlias and hydrangeas, and played "Bananagrams" and "Rummikub" on the beach. Afterwards, we dried off from the outdoor shower with Mom's "just out of the dryer" warm towels. On the way to dinner, we sang along with James Corden in the car, and at sunset, we drank mudslides and ate lobster rolls. For dessert, we bought the last of the nonpareils from the Marketplace candy shop.

On the second morning, Katherine, Laura, and Jayne came back to the cottage with new bikes that had bells and wicker baskets, just like Jessica Fletcher in Cabot Cove on *Murder, She Wrote*. The bikes were painted cerulean and chartreuse and I thought of Antonio, a former student with big marble eyes. He gave color to our school each day. One of his special traits was to see the world in the colors of a Crayola crayon box. My mom, my sisters, my two nieces, and I stood in our bathing suits in front of the new bikes, smiling, the Cape breeze swirling between us, and even if only for a minute, it took our pain and heartache with it.

I lay on the beach and tried to focus on the quiet sounds of the water. One spot down from our blanket, a pair of seagulls had managed to sneak their way into a bag of chips. They screeched mischievously and they dug their beaks into the bag. The mother and daughter lay on the blanket, giggling, their eyes closed in the sun, oblivious of the birds devouring their entire bag of Lime Tostitos. I closed my eyes and wondered where time had gone. How was it possible it was the end of August? Summer had been about intensive care and hospitals, rehabs and skilled nursing facilities, Phil's Green Bay Packers fleece blanket and La-Z-Boy recliners.

Nothing about the summer was lazy.

∾

I couldn't shake the image of Buddy fallen and contorted, gray and wounded. I couldn't go to the basement without hearing his scream. Could no longer picture him walking. My loneliness was so deep that I could not even imagine him with me. When I went to bed every night, I'd stare at the opposite side of the mattress, trying unsuccessfully to conjure up his form.

But that weekend, in the bed by the window, the warm Cape air lulling me back to sleep, I slept on a cloud. I had the same dream two nights in a row.

∾

I walked into Bud's room at Wingate. He sat up straight. "Hey, Ro, watch this!"

He moved his arms. Edged himself closer to the side of the bed. Stretched out his legs, one at a time. Stared at each.

He willed his arms and legs to move, the vein on his forehead bursting. All his energy flowing into his muscles.

"Watch this!" he repeated, his chest puffed out like the king of the jungle.

He looked at me from the edge of the bed. Then looked down to his sneakers. I could see his toes wiggling. Once again, he willed himself to move.

"Are you ready, Ro?" he said.

"Yes, Bud. I'm ready."

He stood, cautiously, wobbling just a bit. He gripped the side of the bed. "I heard you coaching me. 'Find your center. Stand up tall. Head up. Keep it up.'" He thanked me with a smile, then looked back down to his sneakers. "It's time for us to leave."

"I'm ready, Bud. Let's go."

He walked toward me.

Simply just walked toward me. "Take my hand," he said.

And we walked out together.

~

When I awoke, my tears burned my cheeks, my skin so sensitive from all the chemo.

JOSEPH gave me daily reports about what was going on in the solar system. He wanted to fly to the moon and he thought the swings were the best way to get there. At recess one day, on the bench under the tree, I shouted to him, "Fly ragamuffin! Fly!"

"Mrs. Kenner! What's a 'ragamuffin' and how do I know if I am one?"

An avid reader with a rapid-fire brain, he always made me laugh. "Joseph, if someone's my ragamuffin, it's certainly you!"

During testing week, one of the main sections asked the kids to read aloud lists of disconnected words without stopping. As my high-flyer that year, I needed him to score off the charts to bring up the class average. If he appealed for help, it would lower his score.

"'While.' 'Known.' 'Knock.' 'Wrinkle.' 'Strong.' 'Burst.' 'Huss-band.' Mrs. Kenner, what's a 'huss-band?'"

I pointed to my wedding ring, urged him to keep reading. But he was just too inquisitive.

"Huss-band? Huss-band? What's a huss-band?"

I couldn't stop laughing. He was so darling. I kept upping my game with him. I loved that about him. The next day, he came to school wearing a thin T-shirt. There were marks up and down his arms. Eventually, the phone rang and Mrs. Fuller said, "Please send Joseph to the office with his backpack. His mom is here. He's going home."

"You're going home early," I told Joseph. "Have a good day. See you tomorrow."

Mrs. Fuller called back. "You need to pack *all* of his things. Today's his last day." The mom was taking Joseph to her sister's in the Bronx. They were not coming back.

"This is it? This is goodbye? What kind of mom pulls her son out of school in the middle of the day and leaves town?"

A week after I returned from Popponesset, I woke from a deep sleep. I had the most vivid dream about Joseph. In the dream, his mother apologized for pulling him out of Room 4 so suddenly.

"I had to get away," she said. "I had to protect my child."

I woke up feeling penitent. I realized I had blamed the mom all those years. I always thought she had put herself first, that she was being inattentive, but the dream made it clear that she had left the real culprit, the man who had disciplined Joseph with cigarette burns up and down his little arms. She had saved her child by escaping an abusive relationship.

I was sluggish and depressed the rest of the day. Had I been supportive of her? Had I helped her as a mom? I realized I missed something big.

What If I Can't Give You What You Need

For days Daniel and I had butted heads and pushed each other's buttons, so we decided to get outside and have lunch. It was a gorgeous, warm early fall afternoon. We set up the beach chairs at India Point Park. The fall before, Buddy and I had kept the beach chairs in the car and had gone to India Point almost every day.

Daniel came to Providence half of most weeks since Buddy's fall. We had a rhythm of visiting Bud, then family and friends, exercising, and spending the rest of the day planning a fun movie or play and taking respites out in the yard. But that week with Daniel was different. That week was the most stressful. That day was filled with anger. I couldn't get through to him, reach him, receive from him. His typically kind gestures to nurture my weak body and spirit were absent. He held it all in so tightly. I felt like everything I did disappointed him. He closed himself off with a sadness and an anger so raw I worried it would become his new normal. He was exhausted from conflicts pulling him in so many different directions, of being in the wrong place at the wrong time. Leaving, coming, going, staying. Our nerves were raw; deep emotions hit us, colliding into each other, getting us off track. There were profound benefits from being fully present but, by facing the calamity head-on, there was also indescribable heartache and fear.

"I haven't allowed myself to think about hospice," I hesitantly mentioned. "I've put it aside."

"Well, what did you envision this part would be like, Mom?" Daniel asked.

Behind us, a father taught his son how to climb the monkey bars. I slowly enjoyed a turkey reuben from The Butcher Shop and the last of the Cape Cod chips I loved. I thought back to some of the times in India Point Park that brought me joy. I'd bring our Fox Point students to India Point, cross the highway with them on the old shaky bridge. They'd ask me if they could roll down the big hill overlooking the Providence River, and down they'd go, rolling and tumbling and screaming and laughing until they reached the bottom. Once in winter, crossing the bridge, we stopped for a snowball fight, then built snowmen and posed like frozen angels. There had been Fourth Of July Celebrations with Buddy, listening to the Rhode Island Philharmonic, watching the fireworks from the hill. The new Tockwotton Home was across the river and I reminisced about all the years of fun with our grandfriends. I thought of the times we took our fifth graders aboard the *Alletta Morris*, the longest running vessel in Save the Bay's fleet. The students ran to the back of the boat, arms raised gleefully toward the sky, watching their school become smaller and smaller as we motored away down the river. Mrs. Milton and her class raised butterflies from the egg stage. At the end of each year, they'd release them in the park to symbolize their growth.

I thought about what Daniel had said: "What did you envision this part would be like, Mom?" We were both battered by four years of trying to find strength and joy in each day while fighting the horror of our reality. The memories that unexpectedly flooded over me brought a sense of joy, but with them came profound sadness. I was no longer building memories at Fox Point school. I was no longer a teacher. I was a mom, and a wife, on hospice, facing the end of her life.

"My bucket is springing leaks," Daniel said. "I've been carrying a lot of water. And have been carrying more and more and more. So, I learned how to carry more. But now it's busting at the seams. I'm overwhelmed. It's overflowing. And at the same time, and I hate this feeling, I'm relieved that it's leaking. But it also makes me so disappointed that I'm not carrying more. What if I can't give you what you need?"

I took a deep breath, unable to respond, unable to face the possibility that maybe no one could give me what I needed. I thought about Bud sitting in the park, with a book and a Thanksgiving special sandwich, holding my hand. He loved being by the water, resting in the sunshine. I worried I wouldn't be able to give him what he needed.

And finally, I thought of my former student Lynne. According to the substitute, Lynne cried every day during my extended absence in 2013. She worried where I was. She wrote me countless letters expressing her sadness. I hadn't finished doing my job with Lynne. She was so fragile. I hadn't had enough time to help her fully realize her potential in Room 4.

I thought about Daniel, knowing with certainty I wouldn't be able to give him what he needed. I thought about his pain and about how much courage it took for him to voice his vulnerabilities. I understood exactly what he meant. "What if I can't give you what you need?" I had so much love and admiration for him. I let the question lay there between us until it finally floated, unanswered, out over the water.

NICOLE loved going to Tockwotton to help the grand-friends. Once, eager to rush out of Room 4 to celebrate Mrs. Ackerman's one-hundredth birthday, she suggested, "Mrs. Kenner, how about we skip the spelling test today and everyone gets a score that matches Mrs. Ackerman's age?"

A week before Thanksgiving, I was at the grocery store. Nicole's mom was working the checkout. "Can you stay for a few minutes, Mrs. Kenner? Nicole is coming to pick me up. I know there's something she could use your help with."

When she arrived, Nicole came up behind me and gave me a huge hug. "Did you know I'm a CNA, Mrs. Kenner? It all started because of the grandfriends. I'm so glad you're here because I need to ask you a favor. Can you help me get my son into our school?"

She wasn't the demure young girl any longer. My eyes welled with tears. "I'm so sorry, sweetie, but I had to retire because I am sick." Telling her there, at the Stop and Shop, aisle 7, was one of the hardest things I ever had to do. She gripped my hands and started to cry with me. "But, Nicole, honey, how about you call student placement and tomorrow I'll call Fox Point and give Mrs. Fuller a heads-up."

"You were always there to help me, Mrs. Kenner, and here you are."

Later in the week, a colleague called. A first grader had transferred into her class. The son of one of my favorite students.

A Prayer For Thanksgiving

One hundred days into Bud's stay at Wingate and he'd made little, if any, progress toward mobility or independence of any sort. Our goals became avoiding disaster. He suffered from a series of urinary tract infections, pulmonary and platelet issues, and anemia. A severe pressure wound on his back kept him bedridden on an air mattress for October and November. He had physical therapy six days a week at his bedside and was completely dependent on the staff for all activities of daily living. He was absent from the daily social calendar.

Bedridden for fall, one of his favorite seasons. Bedridden for the Brown University football games he loved, where he managed the scoreboard up in the booth, sipping hot soup, indulging in Korb's colossal chocolate chip cookies. Bedridden for trips to the orchard for Macoun apples, for the hundreds of jack-o'-lanterns at Roger Williams Park. Bedridden for a grand-darling's second birthday with Bert and Ernie, for the fall trip to Charlottesville, for hot apple cider donuts and pumpkin carving. Bedridden for all the plays we would have seen at PPAC and Gamm and Trinity. Bedridden for Bob Dylan's Nobel Prize in Literature, for the Cleveland Indians and the Chicago Cubs in the World Series. Bedridden for a historic and polarizing presidential election and his sixty-ninth birthday.

"What're we going to stand up and say about you, Dad, when it's your turn to go?" Daniel asked with gallows humor.

Buddy smiled and considered. "He was a good actor ... a good director…I always loved the students I was working with…Maybe they could talk about the special people I know. That he loved his wife and loved his children and loved having them around. Especially you, Ro," he said, dreamily. "You're the special person in my life. You always know how to put the pieces of my life together. You know what makes me tick."

"That's so sweet," I said. "Thank you for saying that, Bud." In spite of the unbelievable and horrendous challenges we faced, his powerful love and wisdom eased many conflicts each of us felt.

"No, thank you, Ro. For understanding me."

I started to have new, uncomfortable symptoms: intense charley horse spasms in my abdomen and vomiting. Through sixty-three chemotherapy treatments, I never vomited, not once, so seeing all that black bile made me very anxious. The bubbles of air in my bloated gut gurgled like a draining bathtub. Daniel stayed by my bed through the afternoon to help get me comfortable.

"I'm not going to turn the corner," I said to him. "It's not going to get better. I'm learning to be okay with it. I'm not going to have a peak. We have to keep finding the grace in the simple moments. *This* is a peak right now. You plopping my legs up like this…the window's open…there's a fresh ice water and shea butter and yummy dark chocolate by my bed…you positioned my pillows right where I needed them."

"I'm just your little Florence Nightingale," Daniel said.

"This is as close to Heaven as it gets until I'm actually there. I truly mean it."

The next morning, I sat in the living room with my very first teacher friend. She had retired the year before, and we talked openly about the emptiness we felt now that we weren't teachers.

"I'm no longer anyone's superhero," she lamented. With thirty-five meaningful years behind us, we held hands and cried over our cups of ginger lemon tea.

"I look at pictures and I don't recognize myself anymore," I confided. "My body's changing every day and every day I'm pushing it a little more. If I had been this sick the whole time, I wouldn't have made it this far. It's a new stage. I don't want to let anger or regret in, that's just not who I am, but it's frightening when I can't get out of a chair, out of bed, out of the house."

When I was finally able to get back to Bud's bedside for a visit, we sat quietly.

"How are you doing, hon?" he said suddenly. He hadn't asked how I was doing in such a long time. "You're not doing well, are you?"

"No, I'm not feeling well, Bud."

"It's your stomach, right? I can tell."

We talked about Thanksgiving approaching, the foods and people we loved. I began to let myself wonder how we'd celebrate the holiday.

"Will you say a prayer for Thanksgiving, Bud?" I asked him.

"Thank you, God, for all the … for all the … for all the blessed results. Thank you for the vitamins we have in the foods we love. For the peas and the turkey leg … thank you for our blessings."

"Like what? What makes you feel blessed? What makes you happy?"

"I love our physical group. We like to be … we like to be with our group of people eating the foods they love. They make me happy."

"Me, too. And you make me happy, Bud."

"Good. I like being happy, too. Happy is a good thing. So thank you for our family … our family … our people who make us special."

I prayed for the understanding of where, and with whom, I was supposed to celebrate.

"What would you think about me going to Westport to have Thanksgiving with Dianne and Phil, Daniel and my mom?" I asked him. "Then, I'll come home to be with you, Jesse and Ashley, Aaron and Becky, and all the grand-darlings for the weekend."

"I think that sounds like the perfect place for you to rest. Let them take care of you. Come back when you're feeling better."

"Are you sure, Bud?"

"Yes. I'm sure it's what you need to do."

Buddy gave me the soft sense of peace I sought. It flooded my body. From deep inside him, somewhere past the static, he still knew exactly what to say and how to reassure me. In his confinement, he was simply able to be my husband.

Buddy's dedicated CNA came in to feed him dinner. After sipping the hot soup, he looked at me and asked, "Have we ever had pumpkin soup for Thanksgiving?"

"No. I don't think we've ever had pumpkin, or any soup, for Thanksgiving."

"Well then, thank you, Miss, for the delicious Thanksgiving dinner. This has been a nice Thanksgiving together."

After she cleaned him up, she glanced around his room and quietly said, "Give me your hand, I think we should pray…Lord, may the words of our mouths and the meditations of our hearts be acceptable. Please receive our brokenness. Please receive our seeking and our doubting and our believing. Thank you for how you come to be with us, and we do pray that you will show up in time of trouble. That when circumstances can be changed, you change them. And when they can't, for whatever reason, help us understand. We pray for your wings, that when the ground is too rough, we can soar. Pray for this family, bring them into your loving care, and may each of us do our part, as we look to you to do your part. Amen."

Sunset

The night before they left for Charlottesville again after a nice long Thanksgiving weekend, Aaron, the grand-darlings, and I gathered in Bud's room for a wonderful holiday visit. The tension of the past few months dissolved into normalcy. We caught up on Julia's high school senior year, her college applications, and her rehearsals for *Into the Woods*. Isaac was a junior in high school. He'd played in the state soccer championship and was looking forward to upcoming tournaments. Judah recounted his recent second grade field trip to Monticello in amazing detail and told us about his new interest in space and black holes. Ruby was beginning to write plays to share with her cousins and kindergarten friends. Bud complimented each one. We colored with the good Mr. Sketch scented markers and decorated the walls with hearts, geometric designs, and space diagrams. We made Christmas lists, told stories, and watched videos of the kids in rehearsal and Tai Kwan Do practice. Through it all, Bud listened and laughed and smiled at each person surrounding his bed.

"Aaron," he said, "you have an amazing family. You are a good son and a good father. I am so proud of you."

I watched the deep connective bond pass between father and son. Once again, I was reminded how difficult it was for Buddy and his three sons to share a relationship through so many confinements and challenges, but when it mattered most, Bud was able to give his family wisdom and encouragement, pure and simple.

~

A week after Thanksgiving, Buddy and I talked about the four-teen years he taught Performing Arts at Nathanael Greene Middle School. One student from Beth Dolan's class once had a hard time focusing, so she looked to Buddy to help get him motivated at school. Bud invited him to the auditorium and soon learned that the student already knew how to operate and run the antiquated light board.

"Do you remember that boy, Bud? Do you remember that boy you helped at Greene? Do you remember what you told him?"

"I told him if he's going to be here, it's important he's here. He has to be here…he has to be here helping the other kids. That what he's doing is important. It's important to be in school to learn how to be involved in all the programs. Be here and be helpful…be here and be focused for the people that need you…"

That idea lifted, floated, and circulated in the air between us. He was talking about the here and now again.

I hoped people remembered the vibrant and kind essence of Buddy. Many would think back to the good old days at 3 Steeple Street Restaurant, but I thought he'd be remembered most for his work in the theater, on the stage, as a director, and for his work teaching children. Every year, he'd hear from a number of former students letting him know how much he had influenced their lives. And of course, others would know him as the runner on the Boulevard with short shorts and wild hair, or as the legend on the golf course playing barefoot, using only a five iron, an eight iron and a putter; or the uncle with inappropriate jokes. I hoped they remembered Buddy with a sparkle in his eye and mischief in his smile. There certainly wasn't a person who knew Buddy and wouldn't think of him when they heard a Bob Dylan song.

"Hey, Bud," I said. "Remember Daniel's very first Bob Dylan concert? I was nine months pregnant and we were standing in the very first row. I didn't want us to leave, but I was afraid Daniel would be born with a hearing impairment. I made you go out and get the beach towels from the trunk of the car and we sound-proofed my belly."

I looked out the window, the clear sky was a brilliant blue. I tried to remember my very last lesson plan. I imagined I told the students, "Go out and work hard. Have plenty of fun. Read, read, and read. And run in the sunshine!"

I looked at Buddy. "Beth and her student were very grateful to you, Bud. Our family and I are very grateful for all you continue to show us."

"I am grateful to you." He smiled.

"Now," I said, taking his hand, "let's relax. Take a deep breath. Close your eyes with me. Take your mind to the beach. Think about our birds down in Longboat Key. Think about your legs running down the sand and the cool water. The warm sun on your chest. Think of a beautiful sunset and the flash of green on the horizon. Do you see it? Do you feel it? That's where we'll be together."

Jacob 'Buddy' Kenner, November 5, 1947–February 20, 2017
Maureen Kenner, March 6, 1957–March 16, 2017

Dear Future Teacher

MAUREEN KENNER always looked forward to the first day of school. She loved shopping for school supplies, loved getting Room 4 ready, loved sending her summer letter to the students, loved planning the lessons.

It was her thirty-third first day. August 2012. It was very, very hot. She woke up with strange sores on her nose and upper lip. "Oh dear, this is no way to start the first day of school," she thought. "I'm the Teacher from the Black Lagoon." She imagined the children would shriek, "What happened to you? What's wrong with your face?"

There was always so much to do on the first day, yet she wanted to help let the summer joy out, the connections build, the relationships form.

One ritual she had on the first day was to take a picture with all twelve kids under the shady tree. She loved seeing how the students evolved over time. She called them to the bench: "Boys and girls, I want to get a picture." They ran right over, sweating, squishing into each other to get closer to the middle.

Every year, she tried to identify a student to mentor as her ten-year-old future teacher in the making, and Valentina was that person right away. Valentina, Mrs. Kenner's eager, hard-working student for two years, liked to go home, do her homework, and play school. She had a play classroom set complete with chalkboard, desk, and books. Mrs. Kenner and Valentina got along just fine.

That afternoon, while the kids were actively engaged in their groups, Maureen stepped out to the hallway to speak with a colleague. Since Mrs. Kenner was in the hallway, Valentina got up from her desk, glanced at the lesson plan book on Mrs. Kenner's desk, picked up the Reading Street Teacher's Edition, and brought it over to her group. She sat poised in the teacher's rocking chair and read the lessons to the children.

"Lift your pencils and start writing so you don't forget what you're learning," she encouraged them. "Will the fifth graders please help the rest of their friends?"

Out in the hallway, Maureen took her colleague's hand and said, "I'm so proud you're getting the opportunity to witness such a caring, responsible group."

"Now follow my instructions," Valentina continued on to the class. She made a heart with her fingers and held it out to her classmates. "This means I love you, Room 4!"

That last first day photo helped Maureen become less sad about being away from Room 4. It reminded her of how happy she was, how happy the children were. They only got happier and happier as the year went on. Each of the students contributed to making Room 4 such a special place. They grew and they learned so much. They taught Maureen so much.

FUTURE TEACHER, rise and shine, today's your day! Time to pack your lunch, fill up your water bottle, sharpen your pencils, stock up on Mr. Sketch markers and all the new school supplies. Carefully select the pictures for your desk. The love and support from home will be crucial encouragement for you as you begin what I hope will be a long and successful teaching career.

Make room for growth in your tote bag. Find one with lots of compartments, as you'll need to be organized for maximum efficiency. Plus, you'll need hideaway compartments to carefully store all the treasures you'll find. Put these in the prize bag you set up for positive reinforcement. Buy waterproof files for all the articles, photographs, and recipes you will collect for your students. Keep a special spot in your tote for the camera. Have it ready from the first moments of the first day.

Don't forget to charge your battery. Get plenty of rest and fresh air and make time for doing the things you love. Pay attention to how you present yourself. Dress for success. Remember to breathe. Be patient. Your students will mirror your attitude. Their eyes are upon you, taking their cues from you. Try to create a safe and caring environment, a sense of clear and high expectations. Plan rigorous lessons. Consider the multiple intelligences of all the students in your room and have a wide variety of materials to help them show what they know. Always aim for the high-flyers and pair all lessons with fair, consistent, authentic, meaningful feedback. Allow time for the students to investigate and explore concepts in many settings within and around the school. Be proactive. Help your students develop a confidence, an ability to take risks in your class and in life. Let your students know hard work really does pay off.

Take the time to get to know each of your students and their families, their hopes and dreams for the year, their strengths and interests, their family dynamics and support. Find ways you can help make school and learning a positive experience. Reach out to families right away with positivity and personal recognition so you can go to them during the challenging times. And the challenging times will come, over and over again. But, you will have laid the important foundation of a partnership.

Be sure to consistently work on time management. You will be under a time crunch to fit it all in. Maintaining accountability, designing/planning innovative lessons, collecting data, monitoring progress, making accommodations and modifications for your students, writing reports and Individual Education Plans and grants, planning field trips, accepting leadership positions on numerous committees, running after-school clubs, attending professional development, learning new curricula over and over, tutoring, mentoring other future teachers and taking graduate and certification classes…Yes, be prepared for always doing more with less from this day forward.

Make time to build and nurture relationships and partnerships at all levels. You will learn from each other. The more people who love your students, the better. Be open to learning new things to help you, your students, and your community. Be willing to ask for and accept help from other teachers, staff, and administrators. They will become your other family. You will experience much conflict about where to direct your attention and energy. Trust your instincts. Always err on the side of optimism and positivity, even when you find yourself in toxic situations. Be an ambassador for your school, a cheerleader for your students, an advocate for your families. Be respectful of administrators and district leaders; take the time to let them get to know you and your students.

Always put your students first in all your decisions. Be the kind of teacher you would like for your own child, grandchild, niece, nephew, or neighbor. Raise the bar of expectations. It's your job to be proud and boastful for your children. Remember to smile and laugh, or fake it till you feel it.

Be prepared for the hardest work you'll ever love! If you don't find the joy, step back and make some serious decisions, as the children, their families, and your community deserve your very best. Then settle in, ready to nourish your soul, with room to grow and time to thrive. The curriculum will come alive with your flexibility, creativity, and earned support from your team, peers, and families. Trust you are well prepared and able to do this. Have fun! Smile, laugh, listen, and capture those powerful moments. They will inspire you to come back tomorrow and continue for another day.

With admiration, your fellow teacher,

Maureen Kenner

Topics And Questions For Discussion

1. *Room for Grace* is a memoir of a family through the eyes of Maureen Kenner. What do we learn about each member of the family? What do they value? How do they complement one another?

2. What changes do you see in Maureen as she copes with the news of Buddy's dementia versus the way she copes with the news of her cancer? How are they similar? How are they different?

3. How do both Buddy and Daniel deal with the news of Maureen's cancer?

4. Over the course of *Room for Grace*, Maureen experiences many kinds of loss—loss of her life partner, loss of her health, loss of her sense of purpose—which of these is most challenging for Maureen and why? How does her approach to each differ?

5. In what ways do the family express their grief? Who have you lost? How is this story similar?

6. What are some of the experiences Maureen had as a teacher that helped her choose hope over hibernation and happiness over pessimism? How is the world "less scary though the eyes of a

child?" Recall a time you faced a challenge and learned from the children around you.

7. How do you identify yourself? How do you create your identity? How do you identify others? Through work? Personal life? What objects represent you?

8. What is the importance of taking risks? What do we learn about ourselves and others when we take a risk?

9. How does your school/work bring together people who learn and live differently abled?

10. How did Maureen show she could be strong and weak at the same time? Has there been a time in your life where being strong meant letting go?

11. What does it mean to have a moral compass? How does one know if they have a moral compass? Describe someone who does. How do you know they do? What actions have they taken to confirm this?

12. How do you respond to adversity?

13. Describe a person or an event in your life that impacted you to the point of complete reversal of belief. Was there acceptance of a hardship? Clarity to a problem?

14. Who of your family or friends would you like to conduct an oral history with? What are some of your favorite stories they tell? If you began your oral history, what story would you start with?

15. What does it mean to live in the "here and now?"

16. What is grace?

17. What local/national causes or organizations are you interested in learning more about?

18. Write a letter/note to someone that matters greatly to you. Share important memories, what you're proud of, what's hurt you. Share what you want to be carried on after you're gone.

Maureen's Acknowledgments

You are my daffodils, only stronger.

You provide me with encouragement, comfort, and calm during these difficult and extremely challenging times. You help me stand a little taller and let me lean on you when I droop under the pressure. You are my daffodil garden who support and love unconditionally and with abundance.

You are my daffodils who started "Mondays for Maureen" and leave me thoughtful gifts, messages, cards, flowers, and reminders about the comfort and joy that comes with a good book, a cup of hot tea, and a cookie. You are my daffodils who take us out for dinners with pizza and warm cookies or brownie sundaes.

You are my daffodils who sit with me while we watch for hours as the chemotherapy drips into my body. You are my daffodils who bring me to appointments, take perfectly detailed notes, and keep the doctors on their toes. You are my daffodils, my medical team, my Miriam Fain 3 superstars, who tirelessly seek help for your patients. You are my daffodils who text *Just want you to know I'm thinking of you and love you ... Stay strong and positive* right at the very moment I walk home from chemo and collapse in tears. Or to say *Goodnight. Tomorrow will be better.* I wake up and open your texts or letters or cards just as I'm wondering how I'm going to get through it all.

You are our daffodil sons, and daughters-in-law, who make us proud. You are our daffodil grand-darlings who make us smile. You are our daffodil nieces and nephews who continue to share your lives and invite us along for the joy ride.

You are our daffodil oldest friends who never stop trying. You are my children daffodils, who fill my mailbox, and my heart, with your beautiful art, cards, and messages of pure love and concern. You are my daffodils who make me smile when I see you smile, when we meet at the library, in the market, at the theater, in the neighborhood. You are my daffodil support group, brought together under sadness, joined together in love, each of us bearing heartbreaking conditions as we watch our loved ones decline with Alzheimer's and dementia. You are my daffodils who invite us out of the cold and lovingly mull the fresh mint and serve up a tall mojito while we watch the birds and sunset over the Gulf.

You are my daffodils who reach out in prayer, think of me in church, and bring me closer to God in seeking His comfort. You are my daffodils who sit with me, hold my hand, and tell me you're proud of me. You are my daffodils who keep including my family and me in your lives, in your thoughts, prayers, gestures of kindness. You are my daffodils that help me and Buddy and our family find pleasure in many, many of the good days. You are our daffodils … only stronger.

Maureen Kenner
Caring Bridge Journal
March 2015

Daniel's Acknowledgments

Boy, did I get lucky in the dad draft! You have meant so much to me every step of the way. I'm so proud you lived a full life, with amazing glories and stories for the ages. With your dedication to Nan, your grandparents, and to Uncle Julius, you taught me the importance of showing up for family. Through your lifetime friendship with Robert, you taught me to stay loyal and curious. Revealing aspects of your career with Sydney, you taught me the importance of finding a mentor and the reward of taking risks, that art can be cathartic. Through your proud love for Jesse and Aaron, you gave me a dad who wanted to be present for his children's accomplishments. All the best pieces of you coalesced when you became a dad. You taught me about real love through your respect and admiration for Mom. All of your work was earned. You dedicated your life to the truth. I always believed in you and you never let me down. I'm so grateful you taught me the best things of myself. You'll always be by my side. Bob Dylan, Marlon Brando, Lenny Bruce, 49ers for life. Losho Dad.

Mom, I'm so glad you got to meet Jasmine! We just went to Philadelphia to see *Les Misérables* at the Academy of Music. During the prologue, she sat on the edge of her seat, squeezing my hand, and I thought about every time we saw *Les Mis* together as a family. To have shared those deep heartfelt experiences with you and Dad is one of the highlights of my life. I'll never forget Dad reaching out and holding my hand through most of Act 2 while you and I were consumed with emotion, weeping through much of the show. Jasmine and I stood in awe and amazement when the production was over. A feather floated down onto us. And we've been seeing and dreaming of cardinals. Thank you for staying by me. I am so proud of your story. Losho Mom.

My amazing family, with the endless strength and hope you provided, together we continue to experience compassion, laughter, and the thrills of building new memories. From the bottom of my heart, please know your unconditional love, support, and effort continue to make a positive impact on the direction of my life.

To all the students and parents, you are true superheroes, warriors, and winners. It is because of you that Mom grew to learn about fear and empathy, strength and dignity, dedication and perseverance. Your joy and curiosity encouraged and inspired her to keep striving, to keep coming back for another day.

Jasmine, I step into the sun and feel you. When I stumble onto something interesting and astounding, I want to share it with you immediately. You took a past that haunted me and colored it with possibility, patience, and perspective, propelling me with your illustrious spirit and generous nature. Losho.

It was a stranger, a buoyant force of nature, who became the understanding angel I needed to work alongside me. You swaddled me with reassurance, curiosity, hope, and humor. With confidence, I can now let go and share this story. My editor, new hero, my capital W, and companion who has lived one helluvah tale, Annie Lanzillotto.

My trusted draft readers and editors who carried love, tenderness, kindness, and support: Laura Hasler, Leah Plasse, Emily Kunkel, Anna Kruyer, Sam Freel, Ann Hood, Wyn Cooper, Joe Marra, Parisa Zolfaghari, Julia Behar Rolf, Sophia Frank, Ana Giovinazzo, Kate Kennedy, Hannah Bayard.

Many people dedicated their efforts into presenting this book: Jessica Glenn, Robin Vuchnich, Vinnie Kinsella, Katherine Hasler, Nada Sewidan, Deborah Jayne, Ronlee Nemeth, Larry Berglas, Mark Lukach, Laura Yorke, Julia Drake, Volunteer Lawyers For The Arts, Liz Dubelman.

As a son, it's not possible to name and know all people and forces who influenced my parents, but I know they would wish to thank everyone who nurtured and challenged them along the way. With that in mind, I would like to thank:

All the special Foxes, I am forever a better person because you were willing to learn from my mom, to bring her great lessons back into our lives, our home, and our souls: Mary Brennan, Jackie Fish, Ellen Lynch, Caroline Marcello, Patricia Symonds, Charlene Jones and family, Roberta Barros, April Jackson-Hie, Bonnie Clark, Connie and Frank Doyle, Veretta Jungwirth, Lydia Mattera, Sharon Kaufman, Marilyn Dorsey, Holly Polhemus, Mary-Fran Honeyman, Betty Alves, Eileen Afonso, Jane Gross and Al Augusta, Betty Box, Mary McNamara, Emily Teixiera, Sandy Oliviera and Yvonne Smart and the Fox Point Library, Chris Mendonca, David Flink, David Cole, Jonathan Mooney, Maria Ayala, the McEntee family, Gloria Simoneau, Steve Markovitz, Lauri Chung, Jackie Estrella, Lorraine Bibbs, Stacey DeMello, Alison Kupetz, Dianne Maranhas-Boucher, Fritzi Robinson, Joyce Melo, Claudia Pietros, Lisa Vargas Sinapi, Dr. Pia Durkin, Lynn Calcagni, Dr. Lusi, Andrea Mazie, Susan Stambler, Annie Valk, Tom Lester, Betty Lofretto, Michele Carcirieri, Kirsten Murphy, Kris Bradner, Gina Mazza, Kirstin Deshaw, Stephanie Mott, Christy Chase, Melissa Laundry, Catherine Carr Kelly, Tina Cane, Lee Canter, Freddie and Johnny V, Justin Baptista, participants from "Mondays For Maureen" and "Maureen's Garden," principals and office and custodial staff, one-on-one aides, occupational and speech and physical therapists, volunteers, PPSD, Eye to Eye, Tockwotton On The Waterfront, and Brown University Women's Track Team and Brown University Men and Women's Fencing Teams.

The heads, hands, and hearts of all medical care staff: Miriam Hospital and The Fain 3 Cancer Center, Dr. Howard Safran, Dr. Angela Taber, Faye Hollander, Cheryl McGuinness, Irene Kohlberg, Dr. Meghan Nightingale, Dr. Kathleen Higginbotham, Suzanne Gilstein, Dr. David Marcoux, Dr. Derrick Robinson, Dr. Jamheed Vakharia, Rhode Island Hospital NCCU, Mary Ellen Danzer, Dr. Jiao, Dr. Michael Shirazi, HealthSouth Rehabilitation Hospital, Wingate Blackstone Boulevard, Hope Hospice, Glendy, Fruit Hill Day Care Center, YMCA East Side and volunteers.

Friends and neighbors, you never stopped being present with us, witnessing, participating, expressing and sharing love, encouragement, insight and calm: Kevin Miller and Olivia Wong, Alan and Lorrie Handwerger and the Handwerger family, Kate Cox and the Cox family, the Rolf family, Kyle Levasseur, Jay Sackman, the Lavoie family, Sue Greenfield and family, Susan and Scott Haltzman, Marc Bradley Johnson and Amanda Lynn Krieger, Daniel Babigian and Fernando Moreno and River Greene, Qurban Singh Walia, Mac Clevenger, Mike and Abby Jacobs, Peter Schneider and Emma Carhart, Max and Mia Gross, Gabby and Alex Sherba, Troy Philadelphia, Alzheimer's Association, all who donated and walked with *Buddy And Me* and those active participants on Maureen Kenner's Caring Bridge, Monsignor Montecalvo and St. Sebastian's Church, Providence Early Stage Support Group, my Miriam Restaurant family, Yusuf Siddiq, Wrenn Goodrum, Joanne O'Neill and family, Charlotte Duke, Maureen Cohen, Laura Mernoff, Stephen Glantz, Tom

Chandler, all participants at the Christmas Candle Light Vigil and Maureen's 60th birthday celebration, Karen Friend, Kem Fickes, Felix de Voss, Luis Cordero, Meredith FitzGibbon, Joe and Nance Lynch, Bob and Lori Parks, Kathy Flynn, John and Bernadette Redd, Marion Dwyer, Maureen Dolan, Maggie Clegg, Allie McPherson, Gabby Demarco, John Roney, Elisabeth Wilkins and family, Tomoko Shibusawa, Theresa Fox, the Curran family, Molly Lederer, Pat and John Biasuzzi, Jewish Federation of Rhode Island, East Side small businesses, the Bilodeau family, Bob Ducoff, Richard Kaplan, the Ellison family, Alan Wade, Allyson Currin, Elizabeth Kitsos-Kang and family, the cast and crew of *Crave*, BADA, Jill Maybruch, National Players Tour 60, Frank Britton, John Moletress, Washington D.C. theater community, Actor's Equity, SAG-AFTRA, Actors Fund, Labyrinth Theater Company, Frank Vitolo, MaryLee Delaney, Frank Toomey, Barbara LeSavoy, Bob Rizzo, Sarah Morenon, Maribeth Calabro, Marge McCauley, Peter Verrecchia, Doug Jackvony, Dan Cohn, Danny Klau and Mary Knoop, Roman Urbanski, Alliance of Independent Authors, Maisel Deposit Core, Katherine Duceman, David Shepard, Jeremy Clarke, Dayna Sason, Alisha Siegal, Sara Zucker, Caitlin Demerlis, Sebastian Majidi, Erin Hohlfelder, Barbara Grossman, McKenna Schneider, Sophia Blum, and Sarah Chasin.

Work on this book was completed at Harborside Hotel in Bar Harbor, The Central Library of the Brooklyn Public Library, Newport Marriott, Eastern Parkway Library, Drury Plaza Hotel in Santa Fe, Riverbend Hot Springs and numerous living rooms and coffee shops.

Daniel Kenner
New York City
May 2018

About Maureen Kenner

Maureen Kenner's heart was in the classroom. For thirty-five years she was a Special Education teacher in the Providence Public Schools. Born and raised in Dobbs Ferry, New York, Maureen graduated from Rhode Island College with a degree in education and later earned a Master's Degree from Providence College. Maureen was a vital influence at the Vartan Gregorian Elementary School at Fox Point, working tirelessly as a mentor for the betterment of all children and their families. Honored with many accolades throughout her career, Maureen was awarded Providence Teacher of the Year in 2003. Living with cancer, as a model patient, Maureen exemplified integrity, courage, grace, and hope. For thirty-one years, through sickness and health, Maureen was the beloved soul mate to the late Jacob "Buddy" Kenner, her intense love recognized in 2016 as a Rhode Island Caregiver of the Year. www.RoomForGrace.org

About Daniel Kenner

Daniel Kenner rocked out to Bob Dylan's "Knockin' On Heaven's Door" while other infants sang "Mary Had A Little Lamb." A proud member of Actor's Equity, SAG-AFTRA, and National Players Tour 60, Daniel was a Presidential Arts Scholar at George Washington University and Scholarship recipient at The British American Drama Academy. Directed the Washington D.C. premier of Sarah Kane's *Crave*. Author of the manuscript, *Roux*. Winner of the Rhode Island Playwriting Festival for his World War II letters home drama, *Fields of Sacrifice*. Adapted *Les Misérables* for high school stages. www.Daniel-Kenner.com

Help Spread the Word!

Thank you for coming on this journey with us.
We appreciate you taking the time to check out *Room for Grace*.
Two quick favors...

Please tell FOUR friends about this project! More info can be
found at www.RoomForGrace.org

Amazon, Barnes & Noble, Goodreads, etc. all use reviews to
rank books and many readers evaluate the quality of a title
based solely on this feedback from others. Please take FOUR
minutes to leave feedback in their review sections. Even a sen-
tence about what you enjoyed, or didn't enjoy, can really help.